Exploited

Also by Maggie Hartley

Exploited

A TEENAGER TRAPPED IN A WORLD OF ABUSE
AND COERCION. CAN THE LOVE OF A FOSTER
MOTHER SET HER FREE?

MAGGIE HARTLEY

SEVEN DIALS

First published in 2020 by Seven Dials,
an imprint of The Orion Publishing Group Ltd
Carmelite House, 50 Victoria Embankment,
London EC4Y ODZ

An Hachette UK company

1 3 5 7 9 10 8 6 4 2

A CIP catalogue record for this book is
available from the British Library.

ISBN (Paperback): 978 1 409 19746 1
ISBN (eBook): 978 1 409 19747 8

Printed ar~~d bound in Great Britain by~~ S.p.A.

Dedication

This book is dedicated to Hannah and all the children and teenagers who have passed through my home. It's been a privilege to have cared for you and to be able to share your stories. And to the children who live with me now. Thank you for your determination, strength and joy and for sharing your lives with me.

Contents

A Message from Maggie

I wanted to write this book to give people an honest account of what it's like to be a foster carer. To talk about some of the challenges that I face on a day-to-day basis and some of the children that I've helped.

My main concern throughout all this is to protect the children who have been in my care. For this reason, all names and identifying details have been changed, including my own, and no locations have been included. But I can assure you that all my stories are based on real-life cases told from my own experiences.

Being a foster carer is a privilege and I couldn't imagine doing anything else. My house is never quiet but I wouldn't have it any other way. I hope perhaps my stories will inspire other people to consider fostering, as new carers are always desperately needed.

Maggie Hartley

Introduction

Shelley paced up and down the living-room floor, feeling sick from the fear churning in her stomach as every worst-case scenario that she could think of ran on a loop through her head. It would be getting light in a few hours and there was still no sign of her fifteen-year-old daughter Hannah.

Shelley felt helpless and didn't know what to do. She'd tried everything – called the local hospitals, rang Hannah's friends – but no one had seen neither hide nor hair of her. She'd even phoned the police but she knew that realistically a teenager who had sneaked out of her bedroom window to go partying and hadn't come home wasn't going to be top of the list of their priorities. It wasn't as if this was the first time she'd contacted them about Hannah either and she couldn't even say it was out of character anymore.

She must have nodded off on the couch because just before 3 a.m., Shelley heard a crash by the front door. She leapt up to the window and peered out into the darkness. A car, headlights dazzling, screeched off down the street. As her eyes adjusted to the darkness again, she saw someone collapsed on the doorstep.

'Oh my God, Hannah!' she gasped.

As she pulled open the front door, the figure didn't move.

'Hannah!' she repeated, shaking her, desperate to see some signs of life. 'Where the hell have you been?'

Her daughter moaned as Shelley pulled her up to a sitting position. She reeked of cigarettes and alcohol and there was vomit all down her clothes, and her neck was covered in what looked like bites.

'Hannah, where have you been? You've got school tomorrow. I've been worried sick.'

But her daughter was so drunk, she could barely talk.

Using all of her strength, Shelley managed to pull Hannah off the doorstep and into the house. The teenager was as floppy as a rag doll as she heaved her onto the couch. She had done this so many times now, and as a nurse, she knew she couldn't risk putting Hannah to bed in this state in case she choked on her own vomit. So, like countless nights before, Hannah lay passed out on the couch while Shelley curled up in the armchair next to her, barely sleeping a wink, one eye continually on her daughter to make sure that she hadn't been sick and was still breathing.

By the time dawn was breaking, Shelley had given up trying to get any rest. Her youngest daughter Molly would be getting up for school soon and she was due into work that morning. Hannah should also have been going to school but given the state she'd been in when she'd arrived home, it was clear wasn't going anywhere until she had slept off the events of the night before.

As Shelley stood by the window watching the sky slowly turn from inky black to a hazy blue, she made a decision. Her family couldn't go on like this. *She* couldn't go through this again.

Something had to change before it was too late. If something happened to Hannah, Shelley knew she'd never be able to forgive herself. She had tried everything she could to try to control Hannah's wild behaviour and get her beloved little girl back, but now, as she looked down at her daughter curled up looking so dishevelled and vulnerable, she knew there was nothing more she could do. They needed help and they needed it now, before her daughter ended up dead.

ONE

Desperation

The woman sitting in my kitchen was broken. Her hands were shaking as she spoke, there were deep worry lines etched into her forehead and her bloodshot eyes were ringed with dark shadows.

'Do you mind if I nip outside for a cigarette?' she asked.

'Not at all,' I told her. 'I'll open the patio doors for you.'

I led her through to the garden, watching as she lit up. As she took a deep drag on a cigarette, her body sagged with relief.

'I can see she's had a tough time,' I sighed as she paced up and down outside.

'Yes,' nodded Emma, the social worker. 'She's a single mum too, so I think this has been extra difficult for her trying to cope with it all alone.'

I'd never worked with Emma before today. She was small with long dark hair and was so fresh-faced and youthful, I had assumed she must be recently qualified. So I'd been surprised when she had mentioned how she'd worked for another local authority previously.

'Thank you for agreeing to foster Hannah,' she added.

'It's not a problem,' I told her. 'It's going to be hard for everyone but I can see that it's the right thing to do to keep Hannah safe.'

Two days ago I'd had a call from my supervising social worker Becky at the fostering agency that I worked for. She'd been contacted by Social Services about a fifteen-year-old girl called Hannah.

'Sadly it's the kind of case that you and I have seen many times before,' Becky explained. 'Teenager gets in with the wrong crowd and goes off the rails. Hannah's been skipping school and staying out all night. When she comes home, she's usually drunk, and her mum Shelley is worried that she might have been taking drugs too.'

'Is there a boy involved?' I'd asked.

'It seems likely, but we don't know for sure,' Becky sighed. 'Mum has never met these new friends but she doesn't think they're connected to school and Hannah refuses to tell her anything. Shelley has been in touch with the police but she says they're not interested and they don't treat it as a priority as Hannah always comes back in the end.'

Shelley had tried everything to keep her daughter in at night. She'd even got so desperate that she'd locked the girl in her bedroom, but she'd climbed out of the window to get out. Nothing had made any difference so she'd begged her daughter's school for help. As it was a safeguarding issue, the school had been obliged to call in Social Services and yesterday there had been a case conference at the school. The recommendation was that Shelley gave her consent for Hannah to be taken into care voluntarily under a Section 20.

'Understandably she's scared and frightened for her daughter. She doesn't want Hannah to be taken into care but she's at the end of her tether as to what to do.'

I couldn't imagine how this poor mother must be feeling and what a horrendous decision she'd had to make.

'Shelley doesn't have any experience of foster care and what it will involve, so Emma, the social worker, thought that meeting you and seeing the house beforehand might help to reassure her.'

'Of course,' I'd told Becky. 'I'm happy for her to come round if you think it would help.'

Normally my address was kept confidential from parents for safeguarding reasons, but in this case, there were no issues of neglect or any suggestion of Shelley hurting her daughter, so there was no problem about her coming to my home.

So now, a day later, Shelley was here to see where her daughter would be living when she was taken into care.

'Would you like to have a look round the house?' I asked her when she came back in from the garden. 'I can show you where Hannah will be sleeping if you'd like?'

'Oh yes,' she nodded. 'As long as you don't mind, I'd like that.'

As she followed me upstairs, I could see her looking around, taking everything in. I led her into one of the bedrooms that I used for my fostering. The last person who had been in this room was a seventeen-year-old called Rebecca, so it was already set up for a teenage girl. There was a lamp and cushions on the bed and a pretty rug on the floor. There was a CD player and a pile of CDs, and some books and magazines.

'Oh, what a cosy room,' Shelley said, sounding surprised.

'I try to make it as homely as possible for the children who come and stay with me,' I told her. 'I like them to be comfortable and have nice things.'

I think a lot of people have misconceptions about a foster home. They think it's going to be like something out of *Annie* with a line of iron beds – all very bare, cold and basic, but that couldn't be further from the truth.

I showed her the bathroom and pointed out my bedroom and Louisa's old room down the landing. I explained how Louisa had come to live with me when she was thirteen after her parents had been tragically killed in a car crash and that she'd lived with me right up until she was twenty-two. Louisa worked as a nanny now, and she and her husband Charlie had a flat ten minutes away from my house.

'She hasn't lived here for a couple of years so I suppose it's silly keeping her bedroom,' I told Shelley. 'But sometimes if Charlie's away she still stays the odd night here and I'm too sentimental to change things just yet.

'And this is the twins' room,' I went on, as we passed the larger bedroom that I used for fostering. There was a bunk bed and a single bed in there.

Albie and Ethan were seven-year-old identical twins who had come to live with me seven months ago. Their mum Liz had had a breakdown and been hospitalised. Their dad Martin had also suffered with depression and had struggled to cope with the boys alone.

'Thankfully, Liz is doing really well now and the hope is that within a few weeks, the boys might be able to go home,' I told her.

'It's another lovely room,' nodded Shelley.

'As you might have guessed, the twins are football-obsessed,' I smiled. 'I got the football pitch rug from a car boot sale and I got a couple of Manchester United duvets on eBay for the bunk beds. They really love them.'

We walked back downstairs to the kitchen where Emma was waiting.

'It's a lovely house you've got here, Maggie,' sighed Shelley wistfully.

I could see that reality had hit and it was dawning on her that in a matter of days, her daughter would be living here.

I made us all a cup of tea and we sat down at the kitchen table.

'So how am I going to do it?' asked Shelley, her eyes filling with tears. 'When am I going to tell my daughter that I'm putting her in care and she has to go and live with a complete stranger?'

Hannah knew Social Services had come into her school, but she didn't know the case conference was happening.

'Don't worry, Shelley, I can do that,' Emma reassured her. 'I will go through everything with her and explain why we're doing it. You can be there if you want to.'

'I know it will be horrendous, but I think I probably do need to be there,' nodded Shelley.

'She's probably going to be very upset and angry but hopefully in the long run she'll understand that you're doing this for her to keep her safe,' Emma explained gently.

Shelley nodded.

'When will you tell her?' she asked.

'We don't want to do it until the last possible minute,' Emma replied. 'If we give her any advance warning, then there's a risk that she will abscond and we don't want that to happen.'

In three days' time, Hannah's school was breaking up for a week for May half term.

'In a way, it's an ideal time,' continued Emma. 'I can come round to your house on Friday after school and tell her what's going to happen. I'll bring her straight round here and she'll have a week to settle into Maggie's before going back to school.'

'What, she'll have to go straight away, there and then?' Shelley asked.

'I'm afraid so,' nodded Emma. 'If you could have a bag packed for her, that would be brilliant.'

Shelley looked completely stunned.

'I know it's a lot to take in. It's going to be hard, and Hannah will probably be upset and angry, but it's the safest way,' Emma told her.

'Can I come here with her and help her unpack?' asked Shelley, desperately.

'I think it would be better if I bring her on my own,' Emma told her gently. 'But I will make sure that contact is all sorted out so you know you can see her in a few days. Maybe we could arrange for you to call Maggie on Friday night if you'd like that?'

Shelley nodded.

I could see how upset and bewildered she was at the idea of springing this devastating news on her daughter.

'She'll hate me,' she sighed, shaking her head. 'And what about Molly? She's going to be gutted. Despite everything that's gone on, she loves her older sister to bits.'

'I think it's best if you don't mention anything at all to Molly until Hannah has been told,' Emma told her gently. 'I know it's hard but we really don't want to risk Hannah running away or going missing.'

Emma turned to me.

'We've also been talking about schools, Maggie, and Shelley and I both agree that it's in Hannah's best interests not to go back to her current school,' she explained.

'I've spoken to the local education authority and they have agreed to an immediate transfer to a secondary school fifteen minutes from here. Hannah can start a week on Monday after the half term.'

'That sounds like a sensible plan,' I nodded.

'Hannah's going to be devastated,' sighed Shelley.

'I know it's going to be a lot for her to take in but we both know that it's for the best in the long run if we want to try to get her away from this group of people that she's been hanging round with,' Emma told her.

Shelley nodded but the look on her face was one of utter bewilderment.

'Before we go, do you have anything you want to ask Shelley, Maggie?' Emma asked me.

I smiled. 'Well, it would be great if you could tell me a bit about Hannah,' I replied. 'Is there anything in particular that she likes to eat? What does she like doing? What kind of music does she like listening to?'

Shelley shrugged her shoulders.

'Six months ago I could have told you the answer to all of those questions, but now I just don't know,' she sighed. 'She used to love my lasagne and we'd get fish and chips on a Friday after swimming as a treat. She loved dancing in the kitchen with Molly to songs in the charts.

'She liked hair slides and going shopping in town with me and curling up on the sofa and watching a cheesy film.'

Shelley smiled at the memories.

'But now . . .'

She paused.

'Now it's make-up, big gold earrings, mini skirts and cropped tops. She's given up gymnastics and swimming and the only things she's interested in is her phone and how much money I can give her.

'And as for food, she hasn't eaten with us for weeks. I cook but she doesn't come home for dinner and if she is in, she shuts herself in her room and won't talk to me or Molly.

'Everything has changed. Her clothes, her attitude, even her underwear. She's painfully thin.

'So to be honest, Maggie, I can't really tell you anything at all about Hannah because I just don't know my daughter anymore. I feel like I'm living with a stranger.'

'I'm really sorry,' I told her, putting my hand on her shoulder. 'I didn't mean to upset you.'

So often in fostering, I sadly found myself coming into contact with many parents who didn't care about what their children were getting up to, but I could hear the desperation and the worry in Shelley's voice. It was clear that she really loved her daughter and that it was tearing her apart having to have Hannah taken into care.

'It's OK,' sighed Shelley, her voice breaking with emotion. 'I don't know what to do. I've tried everything. I don't know these kids she's hanging around with. I've asked her who they are, if she's got a boyfriend but she won't tell me anything. It's taking its toll on my health now, and her little sister's.'

She described how thirteen-year-old Molly was so worried about Hannah that she was staying awake at night, waiting for her to come home.

'It means she's exhausted too and she can't concentrate in school. It's not fair on her,' added Shelley.

'It's going to be OK,' I promised her. 'I think what you're doing is really brave and by asking for help, I can see how much you care about your daughter. We'll all work together to make sure that Hannah is safe, and hopefully she will start to open up to us about what's going on.'

'That's all I want,' she sniffled, her hands shaking again as she reached for a crumpled tissue to dab her eyes. 'I just want her to be safe and to be able to come back home again.

'I just want my little girl back, Maggie,' she sobbed. 'Do you understand?'

I nodded. But deep down I wasn't sure if that was ever going to be possible.

TWO

The Girl in the Picture

A few days later, I was on tenterhooks waiting for Hannah to arrive. All I could think about was how she was going to feel coming home from school and finding her bag packed and Emma waiting there to drop the bombshell that she was being taken into care. I suspected that, understandably, she was either going to be utterly distraught or furiously angry. My heart went out to Shelley too. I couldn't imagine what it must be like having to pack up your daughter's things and say goodbye to her, knowing that you had agreed to this. It took a huge amount of courage and bravery for her to have asked Social Services for help but even so, I could see from having met her that she was still torn apart by guilt and wondering if she was doing the right thing.

Emma had called me this morning and confirmed that she was going to be at Shelley's house from 4 p.m. so that she would be there when Hannah got home. I needed to let Ethan and Albie know what was happening too.

'I've got some exciting news,' I told them as I drove home from school that afternoon. 'Someone new is coming to live

13

with us later today. It's a girl called Hannah and she might be a bit sad when she arrives so I need you two to be really helpful and watch TV while I talk to her and help her settle in.'

'Is she a big girl or a little one?' replied Albie, who was the more talkative of the twins.

'She's a big girl,' I told him.

'Like Rebecca?' he asked.

Rebecca was the seventeen-year-old girl who had lived with me for a few months earlier in the year. She'd eventually moved to a carer who specialised in looking after young adults like her who had additional needs.

'Yes, she's a teenager like Rebecca,' I nodded. 'But she's fifteen, so a little bit younger.'

Neither of the boys said much else about it. At that age, children just tend to accept things.

When we got home, I quickly made them a snack and a drink. I kept one eye on the clock, wondering when they might be arriving. I didn't envy the task Emma had ahead of her. Would Hannah kick up a fuss or go with her willingly? If she'd had to drag her kicking and screaming into the car then she could be in a real state when she arrived. I really didn't know what to expect.

From my perspective, everything here was ready for her. I'd got some pizzas for tea as they were easy to bung in the oven later on and her room was clean and tidy. All I could do now was wait.

Just after half past five there was a rap on the door.

'Coming,' I shouted.

I stuck my head round the living-room door to check on the twins, who were happily watching TV.

'I think Hannah is here,' I told them. 'I'm going to let her in and have a chat.'

The boys didn't react, their eyes glued to the screen.

I took a deep breath and opened the front door. Emma was standing on the doorstep with a pretty blonde girl. She had a young face but she was heavily made up and mascara was streaked down her cheeks. Her hair was pulled back in a high ponytail and she had big gold hoops in her ears. She was still in her school uniform but her school skirt was the shortest I had ever seen. She was painfully thin, and her pale legs were covered in bruises.

'Hi, you must be Hannah,' I smiled. 'I'm Maggie.'

Her shoulders sagged and she wouldn't make eye contact with me.

'I'm afraid Hannah's a bit upset,' said Emma sympathetically.

'That's understandable,' I told her. 'You've had a shock. Come on in and let's get you something to drink.'

Without saying a word, Hannah followed Emma and I to the kitchen.

I decided I'd introduce her to the boys later on.

'Would you like a drink or a biscuit?' I asked her.

She shook her head, her eyes glued firmly to the floor.

'I know this is a lot to take in, Hannah, but Maggie and I are here to help you,' Emma told her.

She finally looked up, tears filling her blue eyes.

'Too right,' she sniffed. 'Imagine getting home from school one night and your mum telling you she doesn't want you anymore.'

She shook her head.

'I can't believe she's done this,' she sighed. 'She's supposed to love me.'

'Hannah, your mum does love you,' Emma told her. 'And that's precisely why she's doing this. Your mum has asked us for help because she's worried about you. She cares about you and she wants you to be safe.'

'Well, she's got a funny way of showing it,' Hannah replied.

She was unable to hold back the tears anymore and they streamed down her face. It was horrible to see her so obviously distressed.

'Can I go to the loo?' she asked, drying her eyes.

I showed her where the downstairs toilet was while I went back to the kitchen to make Emma a cup of tea.

'That can't have been easy for you either,' I said sympathetically.

She shook her head.

'It was a huge shock for her,' she sighed. 'She was just very upset and in complete disbelief.'

'And how was Shelley?' I asked.

'Doing her best to hold it together but extremely distressed and still worried that she's doing the wrong thing. I said I would pop back later and let her know how Hannah was.'

I really felt for Shelley. It was an unthinkable decision to have to make for any mother.

'And what about her younger sister?' I asked.

'Molly was as shocked and tearful as Hannah,' she sighed. 'She kept begging Shelley to change her mind.'

It was a horrendous situation for everyone concerned.

'Well, hopefully now she's here, things will start to settle down a bit,' I replied.

'I hope so,' nodded Emma.

We both fell silent as Hannah walked back into the kitchen. She'd stopped crying and had wiped the smudges of make-up off her face.

'I've poured you a glass of lemonade just in case you've changed your mind,' I told her. 'You don't have to drink it.'

She gave me a weak smile.

'Hannah, I know you've had a lot to take in today but it's important that I run a few things by you before I go,' Emma told her. 'Your mum and I have laid down a few ground rules for while you're here at Maggie's.'

Because Hannah had come into care with her mother's permission, Emma and Shelley had to decide on things together and present a united front.

'Maggie will talk to you later about bedtimes and what she expects,' she told her. 'Your mum says that you've got a mobile phone and you can keep that, but Maggie will need to have access to it too.'

'No way,' Hannah exclaimed immediately. 'It's not fair that she can just look at my phone.'

'I'm afraid that's what has to happen, otherwise the mobile will be taken away from you,' she told her.

Hannah looked like she was about to cry again.

'For the time being, we expect you to come straight back here after school and you're not allowed to go out at night or drink alcohol of any kind,' Emma continued.

'But what about my mates?' asked Hannah. 'When can I see them?'

'If you want to see them after school, they're welcome to come round here for tea,' I told her.

'I can't believe this is happening,' Hannah sighed, looking furious.

'It's Maggie's job to keep you safe and while you're living here, she needs to know exactly where you are,' Emma told her.

Hannah shook her head and her blue eyes filled with tears again.

'You've got the whole of half term to settle in here and find your feet, and then you'll be starting at your new secondary school,' Emma added.

'What, I have to change schools?' Hannah gasped.

'I know it's an awful lot for you to take in but we've had a chat with your mum and we think it's best and safest for you to have a fresh start at a new school in a different area,' Emma explained.

Hannah looked utterly desperate as fresh tears rolled down her cheeks.

'This isn't fair,' she sobbed. 'Why are you all doing this to me?'

I put my arm on her shoulder.

'I know this feels really hard for you, lovey, but people are actually doing all this because they care about you. It might not feel like it right now, but your mum loves you so much, and she wants what's best for you.'

'That's what we all want, Hannah,' said Emma.

'Well, it doesn't feel like that,' she spat. 'I've been kicked out of my house and now you're saying I'm being kicked out of my school.'

I looked at Emma. I knew that was enough talking for now. Hannah was struggling to take in what we'd told her so far, and she was so upset that nothing more was going to really go in.

'I'll just go and get her bags from the car before I go,' Emma told me and I nodded.

While Emma was outside, I took Hannah to meet the boys. They looked up as we walked into the living room.

'Oh, are you the big girl who's coming to live here?' asked Albie excitedly before I could say anything.

A small smile broke out on Hannah's face at the sight of the two inquisitive little faces looking up at her.

'Yes, this is Hannah, boys,' I told them.

'Hi,' said Ethan shyly, as Albie grinned.

'We're just going to go upstairs so I can show her where she'll be sleeping,' I told them but they were already back to being engrossed in the television.

'They're not normally as quiet as that, I can assure you,' I told her as we waited in the hallway.

'Why are they living with you?' Hannah asked me.

'Children come and live here for all sorts of reasons,' I told her. 'Hopefully Albie and Ethan will be moving back to live with their parents soon, so they're gradually going to be spending more time at home over the next few weeks.'

'What, kids that are in foster care can go back home?' asked Hannah, suddenly looking interested.

'As long as they're safe and happy and Social Services agree to it, then yes, sometimes they can,' I told her. 'Sometimes parents just need to have some help or a little bit of a break and things can change.'

I could see Hannah mulling it over in her mind.

Before we could make it up the stairs, Emma came back in carrying two big bags.

'Here we go,' she said, placing them down in the hall.

'I'm going to go now, Hannah,' she told her. 'But Maggie will look after you and I'll give you a call tomorrow morning to see how you are.'

After I'd waved Emma off, I picked up Hannah's bags.

'Blimey, these are heavy,' I exclaimed as I carried them upstairs, with Hannah following behind.

I pointed out my bedroom down the landing, the boys' room and the bathroom, before we reached the room where Hannah would be sleeping.

'Here's your room,' I told her.

'It'll be weird sleeping on my own,' she sighed as she looked around. 'I'm used to sharing a room with Molly.'

'Would you like me to help you unpack?' I asked her.

'If you want to,' she shrugged.

Shelley had obviously taken a great deal of time and care packing her daughter's stuff. Everything was freshly washed, ironed and neatly folded. She'd covered every eventuality – there was a raincoat as well as a jacket, a pair of wellies, trainers, smart shoes. There were lots of thoughtful touches too, like a book and a dog-eared stuffed mouse toy that had obviously been Hannah's from childhood.

Her face fell when she saw it.

'Why's she put that stupid old thing in there?' Hannah snapped. 'I had that when I was a toddler. Mum always insists on putting it on my bed at night.'

She turned her head away and I could see she was getting upset again.

'Well hopefully your mouse will feel right at home here,' I smiled, placing the toy gently at the end of the single bed.

At the bottom of one of the bags was a photo in a wooden

frame of Shelley, Hannah, and a small blonde girl who I assumed was her sister Molly. I was struck by how different Hannah looked. She was fresh-faced with no make-up, a pink hair slide in her hair and wearing a pretty sundress. They were all eating ice creams with a harbour in the background. Hannah had a big smile on her face and looked so much younger.

'What a lovely picture,' I told her. 'Where were you?'

'It was on holiday in Spain last year,' she said sadly.

I went to put the frame on her bedside table with her book.

'No,' she said firmly. 'I don't want it. Why would I want a photo up of someone who doesn't want me anymore and put me in care?'

'Hannah, of course your mum wants you,' I told her.

But she shook her head, took the photo and shoved it back into her bag.

'I'm going to go downstairs and leave you to get settled,' I told her. 'But before I do, is there anything else that you want to ask me?'

Hannah nodded.

'What do I have to do to be able to go back home?' she replied meekly, suddenly looking much younger than her fifteen years.

'I'm afraid I don't get to decide if and when you go back,' I told her gently. 'That's Social Services' decision, so you will need to talk to Emma about that.

'I know this is all really hard for you and I'm not surprised you're feeling sad and bewildered, but I promise you it *will* get easier. Emma has arranged for your mum to ring me later so you can speak to her then if you want.'

'I don't want to speak to her,' sighed Hannah. 'I just want to go back home.'

I could see we were just going round in circles so I decided to give Hannah a bit of space and time on her own. I went downstairs and put the pizzas in the oven and made some salad. Hannah was very quiet over dinner but she ate a little bit of pizza and the twins chatted about Lego.

After dinner, she sat in the living room, but she seemed oblivious to the programme we were watching, keeping her gaze locked on her mobile and tapping away at the screen. I knew she wasn't going to be happy about it but I made a mental note to check it before I went to bed tonight.

I was in the kitchen tidying up when my mobile rang. It was Shelley.

'How is she?' she asked anxiously. She sounded exhausted.

'She's doing OK,' I told her. 'She's just had some tea. How are you?'

'Not great,' she replied. 'Molly is devastated. She's already told me she hates me and so does Hannah. Do you think she'll talk to me?'

'I can ask,' I replied.

I walked back into the living room where Hannah was still flicking through her phone.

'Your mum's on the phone and she'd love to talk to you,' I told her.

Hannah's face fell.

'Why would I want to speak to her after what she's done to me?' she shouted, storming off upstairs.

Unfortunately Shelley had heard exactly what she'd said.

'She's bound to be angry and in shock but I'm sure she

will have calmed down by tomorrow,' I told her. 'So I'll get her to ring you then.'

But Shelley was clearly devastated and I could hear her sobbing down the phone.

'This is all my fault,' she cried. 'I've done the wrong thing. Maybe I should just let her come home? Maybe now that this has happened, she'll listen to me?'

'Hannah will be OK, Shelley,' I told her gently. 'She's upset and today has been a big shock for her but everything will start to calm down soon. Try and get a good night's sleep and hopefully everyone will feel a bit better tomorrow.'

But Shelley was inconsolable.

'I just feel so sick, Maggie,' she wept. 'Molly hates me, Hannah won't speak to me. I feel like I've failed as a mother.'

'It *will* get better,' I told her.

Today had been a day of high emotions for everyone and I felt pretty drained. Once I'd put the twins to bed, I went to check on Hannah in her room.

'Do you want to come back downstairs and watch TV with me for a bit?' I asked, but she shook her head.

'I'm tired and I'm going to go to bed,' she told me.

'Before you do, please could you leave your phone downstairs charging where I can have access to it?'

She rolled her eyes.

I could see she wasn't happy about it but it was part of the deal that Emma and her mum had agreed on.

'Things will feel a lot better tomorrow,' I promised.

'I doubt it,' she sighed.

To my relief, Hannah did as I'd asked, and when I walked into the kitchen later, her mobile was charging on the side.

Emma had given me the passcode so I glanced through the messages. It all looked fairly innocent. Hannah had been texting her friends about what had happened.

I've been taken into care.

Wat?!! No way. What happened? When u cumin back?

Dunno, she'd replied.

She'd also sent several texts to Shelley.

Please, please can I come home Mum? I promise I will b good. I'll try and come home every night. Please I love u.

Another one read – *Mum why are u doing this 2 me?*

Seeing Shelley's response brought tears to my eyes.

I'm so, so sorry. I love you. Mum xxx

As I went to bed that night, I didn't know what to think. I didn't know anything about these people Hannah had been hanging around with. I didn't know if there was a boyfriend involved or if it was just a new group of mates. Judging from the texts on her phone, it all seemed very innocent.

To be honest, Hannah wasn't the troubled teen going off the rails that I had been expecting. She wasn't bolshie or rude, she hadn't strolled in like she owned the place, sworn at me or answered me back like countless other teenagers had over the years. She seemed genuinely upset about having to leave her mum and sister. It was early days though and I knew my aim was to give Shelley a break and to try to get Hannah into a routine. My job was to make sure she was eating, sleeping and attending school and hopefully, in time, finding out what was at the bottom of what had been going on. Perhaps with someone else in charge and a bit of breathing space, things might calm down and eventually Hannah would be able to go home. But at this early stage, it was the unknown.

Looking at the photo that Shelley had sent, it was clear that the Hannah in bed upstairs was a completely different girl to the one in the picture. That was only a few months ago and the hair, the make-up, earrings and clothes had all changed. Was it just the normal process of growing up, or was there something else or rather *someone* else who was influencing her?

What was clear was that rosy-cheeked smiling girl was gone. My initial instinct was that she was hiding something from us. She had secrets. But the question was, would we ever find out what they were?

THREE

Best Behaviour

The twins were practically bouncing off the walls with excitement, and when I went to check on them, Albie was jumping up and down on the single bed in their bedroom.

'We're going to see our mummy today!' he yelled before leaping off dramatically and rolling onto the floor.

Ethan giggled, clearly impressed with his brother's acrobatics.

'Be careful lovey or you're going to end up at A&E rather than your mummy and daddy's house,' I scolded. 'And please don't try doing that off the bunk bed.'

The twin's mum, Liz, had been in and out of hospital for months after her breakdown but gradually she was getting stronger. She had been back at home for four weeks now, but she was still fragile so we were taking things very slowly. The boys had been having regular contact with their dad, Martin, but this was the first time that they'd stayed overnight at home with both of their parents. They had unsupervised contact, so the boys were going to spend the day with them and then have a sleepover as it was the school holidays.

'What are we going to do while the twins are away?' asked Hannah over breakfast.

'I thought you and I could go to the cinema later today it you fancied it?' I suggested.

Hannah shrugged, looking disinterested.

I had spoken to Louisa the day before, and the family she was a nanny for were away on holiday so I'd suggested that she come along too, as she hadn't met Hannah yet. I also knew that Louisa was usually very good with difficult teenage girls. With her kind, gentle nature, she had a real knack for getting them to talk to her and open up, and my hope was that she could do that for Hannah.

Hannah had been with me for three days now and to my surprise, it had been fairly painless. The weekend had passed quietly. Hannah hadn't asked if she could go out anywhere and she hadn't even moaned when I'd taken her and the boys for a walk in the park and to the supermarket like a lot of teenagers would have done.

Later on that morning, as I was packing a bag for the boys, Emma rang.

'How did the weekend go?' she asked. 'Is Hannah trying to push back against any of the rules?'

'No, not at all,' I told her honestly. 'So far she's been as good as gold.'

'That's great,' replied Emma, sounding slightly surprised.

'What about her mobile?' she added. 'Have you been monitoring it?'

'Yep,' I said. 'Hannah knows I'm checking it and I've said she's not allowed it in her room at night.

'There's been nothing worrying on there,' I added. 'Just a few texts to the same three or four girls.'

'Well that's a relief,' sighed Emma. 'It sounds like the move away from home is already having the desired effect.'

Everything had gone smoothly so far but I wasn't kidding myself. I'd been fostering for long enough to see this for what it was. I knew that Hannah was probably being on her best behaviour in the hope that Social Services would turn around and say there was clearly nothing wrong and let her go home. It was known as the honeymoon period in fostering circles, and whilst some children could only keep up this act for a couple of days, for some it could be a few months before they showed their true behaviours. I was pretty sure that I wasn't seeing the real Hannah just yet, so I wasn't prepared to sit back and let my guard down.

After lunch, it was time to drop the boys off at their mum and dad's. As we pulled up outside their block of flats, both Liz and Martin were there in the car park waiting for us. Liz looked thin and pale, but she'd lost the vacant look in her eyes that she'd had the last time I'd seen her before she'd been admitted back into hospital. Her face lit up when she saw the boys waving at her from the back seat. The second I opened the car door, they both leapt out and scampered into her arms like two excited puppies. They were so energetic and Liz seemed so frail.

'Careful, boys,' I told them gently as I got out of the car. 'You don't want to knock your mummy over.'

'It's OK,' she smiled, clearly delighted to see her sons.

Martin had a big grin on his face too as he gave the twins a hug.

He came over to the car to get the boys' bag out of the boot and looked quizzically at Hannah in the back seat.

'Have you got a new arrival, Maggie?' he asked.

'Yes, that's Hannah,' I told him. 'She's going to be staying with me for a while. She's a little bit shy so I said she could stay in the car,' I told him in a low voice.

'No problem,' he said.

I could see the boys couldn't wait to go up to the flat so we waved goodbye and then drove straight to the café where I'd arranged to meet Louisa for a coffee before the film. She was already there waiting for us.

I introduced Hannah and she smiled shyly at Louisa.

'Did you used to live with Maggie too?' she asked her.

'Yes, I did,' nodded Louisa. 'I lived with her from when I was thirteen until I moved in with my husband.'

'Why did you live there for so long?' Hannah asked, her eyes wide.

Thankfully Louisa was used to the questions and didn't mind.

'My parents died and I had no other family to look after me so I was taken into care,' she replied.

Hannah's face fell.

'Oh, that's really sad,' she said, clearly embarrassed. 'Sorry.'

'It's OK,' smiled Louisa. 'It was a long time ago and I don't mind talking about it.'

Louisa and I had a coffee and Hannah had a hot chocolate and we all chatted about this and that. Soon it was time to walk round to the cinema. As we strolled along the high street, I noticed Hannah kept looking around, a nervous expression on her face.

'Are you OK, lovey?' I asked her. 'Are you looking for someone?'

'No,' she snapped. 'I don't know anyone here.'

'Have you been to this cinema before?' asked Louisa.

She shook her head. 'Never,' she replied. 'We always go to another cinema near where we live.'

As soon as we'd got our tickets for the film, she went to the loo.

'She seems like a nice girl but she's very on edge, isn't she?' said Louisa.

'She does seem very jumpy today,' I agreed, puzzled. I'd never seen Hannah like this before.

Maybe it was the thought of her first contact session with her mum and sister tomorrow that was preying on her mind? Whatever it was, Hannah couldn't seem to relax. She was very restless in the cinema and kept shuffling around, a worried look on her face.

As the boys were away, I made sure the rest of the day was very quiet and we just chilled out at home.

That afternoon, my boyfriend Graham rang. He was a physiotherapist in his forties, and we'd been seeing each other for years now. We both had busy lives and he knew my fostering was all-consuming, so we were both happy to keep things casual. Graham's sister, who lived in Ireland, had just had a baby so he'd gone over there for ten days to see her.

'How's the new arrival?' I asked him.

'Very cute,' he told me. 'Although he doesn't like sleeping much at the minute.'

'Oh dear,' I laughed. 'Your poor sister.'

I explained that I'd had a new arrival of my own while he'd been gone. I told him about Hannah, although for confidentiality reasons I didn't go into much detail about why she was with me. Graham understood that I wasn't allowed to share certain things with him and that I liked to keep my personal relationships and my fostering as separate as I could.

When I came off the phone, I could see Hannah was hanging around the kitchen door.

'Who was that?' she asked.

'That was my partner Graham,' I told her. 'We don't see each other that much and he's been away for a little while.'

'Does he come round here?' she asked.

'Sometimes,' I told her. 'But not when foster children are around.'

It suddenly struck me that this was a good opportunity to ask her a few questions and do some digging.

'You're being very nosey,' I teased. 'Have you got a boyfriend then?'

Hannah's face went beetroot red.

'No,' she snapped. 'Why? Who told you that?'

'Nobody,' I replied. 'I just wondered.'

'Well it's none of your business,' she told me.

She looked upset and I could see it was clearly something she didn't want to talk about.

I quickly changed the subject.

'Remember your mum and Molly are coming round tomorrow morning,' I told her.

Her face softened. 'Oh yeah,' she said.

I wasn't sure how she was going to handle seeing them.

That night Hannah went to bed early and with the boys away and no bath and bedtime to do, I made sure that I took advantage of an early night too. But when I actually got into bed, I couldn't sleep. I lay there, tossing and turning, my mind racing. I thought about the twins and how they were getting on sleeping at home for the first time in eight months. I also worried about Hannah and how tomorrow's contact session was going to go.

In the end I sat up. The glow of my alarm clock told me that it was 1 a.m.

I was wide awake and now I needed the toilet. I got out of bed and pulled on my dressing gown. As I padded down the landing towards the bathroom, I realised I could hear something. I stopped and listened again.

It sounded like somebody talking.

It was muffled but I could definitely hear it. The more I listened, the more I was sure that the voice was coming from Hannah's room but I couldn't see any light coming from under her door, and I knew her phone was downstairs, charging, because I'd seen it before I came up to bed. The floorboards creaked as I crept along the landing in the dark and suddenly the voice stopped. I hovered outside Hannah's door and listened, but it was all quiet. Her bedroom door was slightly ajar so I pushed it open and peered around. I could see Hannah's blonde hair on the pillow and the duvet rising and falling with her breath. She was fast asleep.

I'm so tired I must have imagined it, I told myself.

After I'd been to the bathroom, I went back to bed and thankfully I must have nodded off too. The next thing I knew, my eyes flickered open and I glanced at the clock. I leapt out of bed in a panic when I saw the time.

It was 8.30 a.m. Normally the boys woke me up by seven, but it was quiet without them here and there was no school run to do today. When I went downstairs, Hannah was sat in the kitchen having some cornflakes.

'I'm sorry I slept in,' I told her. 'It's not like me. I've not done that in years.'

'It doesn't matter, does it?' she said. 'We don't have to be anywhere.'

'No, I suppose not,' I said, flicking the kettle on wearily.

Shelley and Molly weren't coming round until after lunch, so I sat down at the table with my cuppa.

'A weird thing happened last night,' I told her. 'I got up to go to the loo in the middle of the night and I could have sworn I heard a voice coming from your room.'

'My room?' she said, looking down at her cereal. 'That's strange. I wasn't talking to anyone. You must have been hearing things.'

She paused.

'Oh I know,' she said suddenly. 'I bet I was talking in my sleep. Molly says I do it all the time and it drives her mad.'

'Maybe that's what it was,' I smiled.

We had a quiet morning at home. I could see Hannah was nervous about seeing her mum and sister. Emma was going to give them a lift over here early afternoon.

After lunch Hannah spent most of the time hovering by the living-room window, biting her nails and looking anxious.

'They're here!' she shouted just after one o'clock.

I went to the door to let them in while Hannah hung back nervously in the hallway. Emma was doing her best to keep everyone upbeat.

'Hi Maggie,' she said cheerfully. 'If it's OK with you, I'll just come in for ten minutes and make sure everyone is OK?'

'Of course,' I told her.

I said hello to Shelley, who looked nervous, and introduced myself to Molly. She was a sweet girl who had the same blonde hair as her sister. She smiled shyly when she saw Hannah, both girls seemingly unsure what to do or how to act. I noticed Molly's arm was in a plaster cast.

'Oh no,' I gasped. 'What have you done to your arm?'

As soon as Hannah heard this, she shot over to her.

'What happened, Moll?' she asked, her face creased with concern.

'Some idiot pushed past her on the way home from the park after school and knocked her onto the road,' tutted Shelley. 'She was lucky there wasn't a car coming. She fell on her arm and broke it.'

'Oh my God, Molly,' gasped Hannah. 'You poor thing. I'm so sorry.'

'It's OK,' replied Molly. 'At least it gets me out of PE for a few weeks.'

But Hannah looked really upset about it and I could see she was close to tears.

We were all still lingering in the hallway.

'Let's go and sit down in the living room,' I suggested.

I could see Shelley and Molly were nervous about being in someone else's house and were unsure what to do so I wanted to make them comfortable.

'How are you, love?' Shelley asked Hannah nervously as we all sat down.

'I've been really good,' she replied eagerly. 'Maggie, will you tell her? I've done everything that she's asked so please can I come home now?'

Shelley gave Emma a panicked look, and it was clear she had no idea what to say.

'Hannah, this is just a contact session where your mum and Molly have come round to see you and spend time with you,' Emma told her gently. 'It's not about going home. That's not even up for discussion at this point, I'm afraid. It's very early days and we're still working things out.'

'Well, what are we supposed to do now then?' asked Hannah, looking perplexed. 'Are we going out somewhere?'

Emma shook her head.

'Not this time. We thought it would be nice to have the contact here today so your mum can see how you are and that you've settled in OK.'

'But I've not settled in,' sighed Hannah. 'I just want to come home.'

It was clear Shelley was struggling to know what to say and I could see she was getting upset.

Thankfully Molly stepped in and managed to change the subject.

'Where do you sleep?' she asked her big sister. 'It's weird not having you in our room at night.'

'Can I show Molly my bedroom?' Hannah asked.

'Yes of course, that's fine,' I smiled.

The two girls went upstairs and I could hear them chatting away. Hannah was still questioning Molly about her broken arm.

'Why don't we leave them to it and go into the kitchen and have a cuppa?' I suggested.

Shelley nodded, looking relieved. Understandably, she seemed to be finding this very hard so I did most of the talking. I told her that the last few days with Hannah had gone well and explained that Ethan and Albie had stayed overnight with their parents and wouldn't be back until later. I also mentioned that we'd been to the cinema. She sat listening, but she looked fairly shell-shocked.

'Well I think I'll leave you to it,' said Emma, finishing her tea and getting up. 'I'll be back in an hour or so. Does that seem long enough?'

Shelley shrugged. 'It should be,' she said. 'This is all very new to me so I'm not sure what we should be doing at these sessions.'

'You don't have to do anything,' I told her kindly. 'There are no rules. It's just a chance for you to spend some time with Hannah and hopefully put your mind at rest that she's doing OK. I know it feels awkward this time, but as time goes on it will get easier.'

I saw Emma out. The girls were still upstairs so I went back to the kitchen to sit with Shelley.

'So how's Hannah been?' she asked anxiously. 'Has she been asking to go out at night?'

I shook my head.

'No, she's not mentioned it,' I told her. 'She's been messaging her friends on the mobile but I've been checking it every night and I've not seen anything that's worried me. It's just general chit chat between the same three or four girls.'

Shelley looked relieved but confused.

'Do you think the problem was me?' she asked, her brow creased. 'Do you think I handled it wrong?'

I explained to her about children adapting their behaviour when they first come into care in an effort to put her mind at rest.

'So Hannah's been eating OK and sleeping well?'

'Absolutely fine,' I told her. 'Although she was talking in her sleep last night, but she said she often does that.'

Shelley looked puzzled.

'Really?' she laughed. 'I've never heard her do that.'

'She told me Molly said she did it all the time,' I replied.

But before I could ask any more questions, the girls suddenly appeared.

'Hannah's bedroom's really nice, Mum,' Molly told her.

'I know,' she replied. 'Maggie's got a lovely place here.'

'What should we do now?' asked Hannah.

I could see none of them were sure what to do.

'Han, can you paint my nails?' Molly asked her.

'Sure,' she said. 'I've got some polish in my room.'

I suggested they all go into the living room where they'd be more comfy.

'I've got a few jobs to do around the house so I'll leave you all to it,' I told them.

I went out of the room although I lingered in the hallway, sorting out some of the boys' coats so I could keep one ear on what was going on. As far as I could tell, there wasn't much interaction between Hannah and Shelley. It was clear that Hannah was still hurting about being taken into care. She needed someone to blame and Shelley was taking the brunt of that. To my relief, the girls at least seemed to be chatting away to each other happily enough.

I could hear Molly telling Hannah about something that had happened at school as Hannah painted her nails for her.

'How are you feeling about starting at the new school next week?' Shelley asked.

'Rubbish,' she snapped. 'I don't want to go to a new school but thanks to you I have to.'

'Hannah, you know I just want you to be safe,' Shelley told her. 'Those people you were hanging around with were leading you astray and you were missing so much school.'

'This is all your fault,' Hannah spat. 'It's your fault that I'm stuck here.'

Things were quickly turning sour and I knew I needed to intervene.

I popped my head around the door.

'Anyone ready for another drink?' I asked in a bid to try and diffuse the situation.

'Yes please,' said Shelley, clearly grateful for the interruption.

She jumped up and collected all the dirty mugs.

'I'll bring these into the kitchen for you.'

She followed me into the kitchen and put the cups on the side.

'I don't blame her for giving me a hard time,' sighed Shelley, her eyes filling with tears. 'I still feel so guilty that she's here.'

'I know it's hard and you're bound to feel guilty, but what you've got to remember is that Hannah has been absolutely fine so far,' I reassured her. 'And if she hadn't, then I promise you that I would tell you.'

Shelley started to cry.

'What makes me feel even more guilty is that it's been a relief,' she sobbed. 'For the first time in months I've had a proper night's sleep.

'I miss Hannah, of course I do, but it's so nice not to have to worry about where she is and whether she's going to come home and have to phone the police.'

'That's completely understandable,' I said, putting my arm around her. 'No one can live like that.'

Once she'd calmed down a bit, I made us another cup of tea and then took her back to the living room. To my relief, the three of them spent the rest of the time playing cards, and there were no more arguments.

Time passed quickly and before long, Emma was back at the door.

'We need to sort out next week's session,' she told us.

I wanted to try to time the contacts to coincide with when Ethan and Albie were away so I could give Hannah, Shelley and Molly my full attention. As long as everything had gone well, Ethan and Albie would now be having regular sleepovers at home once a week. Liz and Martin were going to pick them up from school on Wednesday, then take them to school the following morning.

'Could you do next Wednesday when Hannah gets back from school?' I asked.

'Yes, I can come round after work,' nodded Shelley.

Then it was time to say goodbye.

I could see Hannah was doing her best not to cry as she gave Molly a hug.

'Look after yourself, Moll,' she told her. 'Please be careful. I hope your arm is OK.'

It was Molly's turn to get teary.

'It's not fair, Mum, why can't Hannah come back with us?' She pleaded. 'She doesn't live here, she lives with us.'

I could see Shelley was getting upset too.

'It's not a simple as that Molly, love. Remember all those nights you and I were up worrying about where Hannah was?

You weren't sleeping and you were so tired at school, you were getting into trouble. We couldn't carry on like that.'

'Yeah, but if she comes home then she wouldn't do that anymore, would you Han?'

'She has to stay here for now,' said Shelley firmly, though I could see how much it pained her.

She turned to Hannah.

'I know you don't believe it, but I love you, Hannah, and we'll see you soon,' she told her.

But when she tried to put her arms around her for a hug, Hannah shrugged her off.

'Keep in touch,' I told Shelley, giving her a sympathetic smile.

After I'd waved them off, I closed the front door.

Hannah was standing with tears in her eyes.

'I know that was hard, lovey. It must feel really strange seeing your mum and sister and not going home with them, but next time will be easier, I promise,' I told her.

'There won't be a next time,' she told me decisively. 'I don't want them to come round on Wednesday and I don't want to see them anymore. I want you to ring Emma now and tell her.'

I was shocked at this sudden response.

'I know you're still angry at your mum about what's happened, Hannah, and I understand that, but I'm sure you'll change your mind in time,' I told her.

'No,' she said firmly, shaking her head. 'I won't change my mind.'

From the tears in her eyes, I could see she was upset but it was also clear that she was very determined. I wondered what had caused her to react like this. From what I'd seen and heard, it had seemed as if she and Molly had got on really well.

'I never want to see either of them again,' she cried, before running off upstairs.

For now, I knew I had to respect her wishes. As I heard Hannah's bedroom door slam, I knew there was nothing I could do to make her change her mind.

FOUR

Clues

Hannah shuffled uncomfortably in her seat. We'd come to meet the head teacher of her new secondary school and I could tell by the look on her face that she was nervous. Ms Hicks had kindly agreed to come in and see us during the holidays so that Hannah could start straight away on the first day of term.

Previous foster children had attended this secondary school but back then it had been under the old headteacher who had now left so this was the first time that I'd met Ms Hicks. She was a dynamic Scottish woman in her late forties.

'Well Hannah, I've been going over your records from your old school,' she said. 'Up until four months ago you were doing really well. Your attendance was excellent, you had a positive attitude to school and your predicted grades were good. What on earth happened?' she asked, peering over the top of her thick tortoiseshell glasses. 'What's changed?'

Hannah shrugged her shoulders and stared at the floor.

'If you come to this school then we will expect you to knuckle down,' she said firmly. 'I want to get you back on track but we need you to be on board and willing to work. Your GCSEs are a year away yet, and there's no reason why you can't do well in them. But for that to happen, you need to get your head down, work hard and come to school every single day. Do you understand?'

Hannah nodded sheepishly.

'Thank you for coming in during half term to see us,' I told her.

'My pleasure,' she smiled. 'I'm keen that Hannah doesn't miss any more school. I've printed out her timetable and you have her tutor's details so you can contact us at any point.

'And are you all sorted for uniform?' she added.

'We're just about to go to the uniform shop in town and pick up a few bits,' I told her.

'Good,' she said. 'We look forward to seeing you on Monday then, Hannah.'

Hannah was very quiet as we walked out of the school building and into the car park.

'Well?' I asked her. 'What did you think?'

'It was OK,' she sighed. 'She seems a bit strict.'

'Oh I quite liked her,' I said. 'I think she's exactly what you need.'

We got in the car and headed to town. My friend Carol, who was also a foster carer and lived a few streets away from me, was keeping an eye on the boys along with her three foster children, Mary, Dougie and Sean, which meant that Hannah and I could go shopping for the things she would need for school.

'It'll be OK you know,' I reassured her as we drove along. 'I know you're nervous but you'll soon make new friends.'

'I don't see why I have to go to that stupid school,' she sighed.

'Emma and your mum agreed that it was for the best,' I told her.

I knew it was a lot of change for her to cope with but everyone agreed that she needed a fresh start.

Luckily Hannah's new uniform was similar to her old school. Shelley had packed several white shirts and grey skirts so all we needed was a blazer, a couple of jumpers and a tie, so we got everything sorted quickly.

When we got back, I chatted to Carol while Hannah went straight on her mobile. She came running over to me.

'Maggie, can I go and meet my friends in McDonald's this afternoon?' she asked.

'Hmm, I'm not sure about that,' I told her. 'Remember what Emma said about you not going out on your own?'

'But I haven't been anywhere since I came here and it's the middle of the day,' she pleaded. 'I'll only stay an hour and I promise I'll come straight back. Look, you can check my phone if you want. There are texts on there from Lizzie and Martha.'

She shoved her mobile into my hand and I scrolled down. Sure enough, there were messages back and forth about meeting at a McDonald's in a nearby town. Lizzie and Martha were names I recognised from previous texts that had all seemed pretty innocent.

'I tell you what, let me give Emma a call and I'll check it with her,' I told her.

She looked ecstatic that at least it wasn't an outright 'no'.

When Carol had gone and the boys were happily playing with some Lego, I went upstairs out of earshot of Hannah and gave Emma a ring.

'I know you said no going out, but it's the middle of the day, and I recognise these girls' names from her texts and I would drop her off and pick her up,' I told Emma. 'It's normal behaviour for a girl her age to want to meet her friends and I think she could do with a bit of normality.'

'How's she been the rest of this week?' Emma asked.

'Absolutely fine,' I told her honestly. 'She's been stuck in the house for most of the week. To be honest, Emma, if she did want to go out I can't actually stop her. She's fifteen, so I can't physically restrain her and force her to stay in.'

'OK then,' she said. 'I suppose we have to start building some trust.'

So far Hannah hadn't done anything for me not to trust her. When children come into foster care there's a lot of behaviours they leave behind because they're connected to people, so the way Hannah responded and reacted to me might be different to the way she responded to Shelley.

Hannah was ecstatic when I told her that she could go. It was the happiest that I'd seen her all week.

'I'll drop you off at McDonald's, then I'll come and pick you up,' I told her.

'But I'm not a baby, I'm fifteen,' she sighed.

'I know, but I need to take the boys into town anyway to do some shopping so this is the ideal opportunity,' I told her. 'It's your choice. You can either do it this way or not at all.'

'OK,' she sighed.

She probably thought I was being a bit harsh but it was important for Hannah to know that she had to follow the rules laid down for her.

Later that afternoon, we all drove into town. I pulled up into a parking space where I could see the entrance to McDonald's.

'We'll come and get you in a couple of hours,' I told her firmly. 'Have your phone on just in case.'

'OK,' she said.

I could see she couldn't wait to be off. I watched her walk across the street towards McDonald's where I saw two girls waving at her. They all hugged each other and walked in. Everything looked exactly as she'd explained it.

However, this was also the first time that she had gone out alone while she'd been at my house and it was the perfect opportunity for her to meet up with the person or the people who had led her astray. I suspected from the texts that I'd read that it wasn't Lizzie or Martha who had been a bad influence, but I didn't really know Hannah. I just had to put my trust in her that she was telling me the truth.

The boys and I wandered around the shops and they managed to persuade me to take them into a toy shop. As we traipsed up and down the aisles, my mind kept flicking back to Hannah. Had she stayed in McDonald's? Was she still where she said she was with Lizzie and Martha or was this all a big ruse so she could go and meet someone else?

I'll soon find out, I thought, as we walked across town to collect her a couple of hours later. I felt strangely on edge as we approached McDonald's. I wanted to have faith in Hannah but a little part of me wasn't expecting her to be there. So I was surprised when I saw her waiting outside with the two girls I'd seen earlier.

'Is that her?' I heard one of them say as we walked over to them.

'Yep,' she nodded. 'That's Maggie.'

She looked embarrassed and I could tell she didn't want to introduce me to them so I had to respect that. I gave her a wave and the boys and I crossed the road and got into the car and waited. Hannah said her goodbyes and came over to join us.

'Did you have a nice time?' I asked her, once she'd climbed in.

'Yeah, we had a milkshake and just chatted,' she nodded.

As soon as I got home, I settled the boys in front of the TV and went upstairs and called Emma.

'What's happened?' she asked anxiously.

'Nothing at all,' I told her. 'It all went perfectly. Hannah was where she said was going to be, with who she was supposed to be with. Everything was fine.'

'Oh good,' she said.

Maybe we had all got it wrong and this was what she'd needed – to get away from the bad crowd who had been leading her astray, whoever they were, and cut ties with them.

Before I knew it, half term was over and it was Hannah's first day at her new school. As she stood by the front door in her new uniform, she looked terrified.

'It's going to be OK,' I reassured her, as I had many times before to various children in my care.

I'd agreed that I'd drop her off each morning to make sure that she was actually going in. I'd worked out that I could get her there for 8.20 a.m. and still manage to get Ethan and Albie to their primary school on time.

'It's really embarrassing you taking me in,' she moaned as we pulled up outside the school. 'What if people see you?'

'I don't care,' I told her. 'I want to make sure that you're here safely and you don't know the area yet.

'I hope you have a good first day and you've got your mobile so ring me if you're lost or running late tonight.'

'I will,' she huffed, rolling her eyes.

I really did sympathise with her. I knew it wasn't easy moving schools as a teenager when everyone already knew each other.

All day I was on tenterhooks, thinking about her and wondering how it had gone. I was hovering by the door when she got in just after 4 p.m.

'How was it, flower?' I asked her.

'Okay, I suppose,' she replied. 'It's really big.'

'What are the other pupils like?' I asked her.

'They seem alright,' she said. 'I didn't really talk to anyone though.'

On the face of it, her first week seemed to go well. I dropped her off every morning and every night she was home at the same time.

When I'd checked Hannah's phone, I could see that Shelley had regularly been texting her. She'd wished her goodnight and asked how school had gone although Hannah had never responded to her messages.

Hannah was still adamant about not wanting any more contact.

I'd told Emma that Hannah had said she didn't want to see her mum or Molly anymore and she had told Shelley. Understandably she was devastated.

'I explained that it was probably Hannah's way of punishing her for putting her in care,' Emma had said. 'And I was sure she would change her mind eventually.'

But so far, there was no sign of a change of heart.

During Hannah's second week at her new school, I was on a training course for three days. On the first day, I turned my phone on at lunchtime to find that I had a missed call and a voicemail. It was from a Mr Granger – the deputy head of Hannah's year – asking me to give him a call. I rang him back straight away.

'Thanks for ringing,' he told me. 'I just wanted to check something with you. We've noticed that there's been a few times where Hannah has missed a couple of lessons in the middle of the day. I can see from her records that she's recently come into the care system and I wondered whether she had been going to any appointments?' he added.

'No, not at all,' I told him, alarm bells starting to ring. 'If she had any appointments, I'd have contacted the school and come and collected her and signed her out. What has she missed?'

'She missed two lessons on Wednesday and Friday of her first week and then two on Monday of this week. It's taken us a while to realise because it's different subjects with different teachers and she was there for registration at the beginning of the day and in school at the end of the day.'

I couldn't help but feel suspicious. Was Hannah up to her old tricks again?

'Thank you for letting me know,' I told him. 'Let me have a word with Hannah tonight and I'll give you a call back.'

I honestly didn't know what to think. I'd dropped Hannah off at school every morning and watched her walk in through the gates. Mr Granger had said she was always there at the end of the day. So if she was in school, why on earth was she missing lessons?

'School rang me today,' I told her casually when she got in that evening. 'They said you'd missed a few lessons in the middle of the day. They said it happened twice last week and once this week.'

I paused. 'Where were you, Hannah?'

A panicked look flashed across her face.

'I got lost,' she said meekly. 'I couldn't find the classrooms where I was supposed to be and I was just walking around and around in circles and getting more and more panicked. So I went to the library and sat in there instead.'

'If you were lost, lovey, then why didn't you ask somebody for help?' I asked gently.

'I felt stupid,' she replied. 'I hate being the new girl when everyone else knows where they're going. I got really upset. I knew you'd be cross with me so I didn't say anything.'

'Hannah, I wouldn't be cross with you,' I told her. 'I'm on your side. It's bound to be difficult because everyone else has been there for years. I know it's hard being the new girl but you've got to ask people for help.'

I sympathised with her. I knew I would feel anxious if I couldn't find the right room and was wandering around aimlessly. I'd also fostered older children in the past who had done the same thing. They were too embarrassed to walk into a lesson late so they'd hidden in the toilets or somewhere around the school. Given Hannah's prior history of truanting, I couldn't suppress a small niggle of suspicion, but I decided to give her the benefit of the doubt.

'You're doing really well,' I told her. 'But you can't skip two hour-long lessons. Remember what the head said – she wants 100 per cent attendance. Mr Granger said he'll be keeping a close eye on it and he'll ring me if it happens again.'

Hannah nodded. She looked really upset and I didn't want to push it too far. She had been through a lot in the past few weeks.

I called Mr Granger and let him know what had happened and I also logged it in my daily notes so my agency and Emma would know what had happened.

Thankfully by Hannah's third week things seemed to have settled down.

'There's an athletics club tomorrow night after school,' she told me one evening over tea. 'Can I go?'

She hadn't done any extra-curricular activities so far and I was keen for her to get involved as it was a good way to make friends.

'It sounds good,' I nodded.

'It's at a stadium near school and it doesn't finish until half past five so by the time I get the bus I won't be back until after six,' she told me.

'I can come and pick you up if you want?' I suggested.

'No, you'd have to bring Ethan and Albie,' she told me. 'I'm alright getting the bus. I know where I'm going.'

The evenings were light now and I had to allow her some element of freedom.

'OK,' I told her.

I wanted to trust her, but as a foster carer, I also had to cover my own back. The next day, I gave the school office a quick call and they confirmed that a new athletics club was starting after school. I was relieved.

The following evening, I was playing snakes and ladders with the boys. They were tired after school so I'd decided to give them an early tea. Hannah and I could eat later when she got in. But at six o'clock I got a text from her.

Had to wait ages for the bus. On 1 now. Will be a bit late.

Poor love, I thought to myself. She's had a long day.

No probs. See you soon. I messaged back.

It was 7 p.m. before Hannah walked in the front door.

To my surprise, she was in her school uniform rather than her PE kit, and she looked pale and exhausted.

'How was it?' I asked her.

'Good,' she shrugged. 'They train twice a week so can I go on Tuesday as well?' she asked.

'I don't see why not,' I smiled.

'How come you're not in your PE kit?' I added.

'Oh, I was cold, so I wanted to get changed,' she replied.

It was good to see her getting involved. The next time I texted Shelley I mentioned it in my message.

Wow, athletics really?? she'd said along with a surprised emoji. *She's never been interested in sport before.*

For once, everything seemed to be going smoothly and as a foster carer you have to savour those little moments of calm because they don't happen very often. However, I wasn't naïve. Given Hannah's history, I was still checking her phone every day and looking out for anything suspicious, but to my relief, I hadn't found anything to misplace my trust. Hannah appeared to be settling in at school and everything was going brilliantly with Albie and Ethan. The regular sleepovers with their parents were going well and a few days later we held their Looked After Child review. This was a meeting where everyone involved in the boys' care – their social worker, birth parents and their teachers – got together to work out a long-term plan for their future.

It was being held at my house during the day when the twins and Hannah were at school. As I tidied up the living room before the meeting, I felt a flutter of nerves in my stomach. I knew this was an important meeting, as today was decision day for the boys. Their social worker Mandy had to decide whether to start the process of moving the boys home so they could live permanently with their parents again.

When Liz and Martin arrived, I could see they were nervous. Mandy was an experienced social worker and she did her best to put them at ease.

'How's it all going?' she asked as I poured cups of tea and passed round a plate of custard creams.

'Fine,' said Martin. 'We're loving having the boys back home overnight and they seem happy.'

She turned to Liz who had been quiet since arriving.

'How are you feeling about it?' she asked her. 'Do you feel like you're coping being back at home?'

'Honestly, I really am,' she said. 'Martin's been brilliant and I'm enjoying being their mummy again. It breaks my heart when I have to say goodbye to them. The house feels so quiet without them rushing around and chattering all the time.'

Mandy was nodding and taking notes.

'How are things going from your perspective, Maggie?' she asked me. 'How are Ethan and Albie doing?'

'They're sweet, happy little boys,' I smiled. 'They're excited to see Mummy and Daddy and they talk about them all the time. Not as much as they do about Manchester United, but almost as much.'

Liz and Martin laughed.

'They just seem very content,' I said. 'And from my perspective, even though I'm going to miss them, I can't see any reason for them not to be able to go back home.'

Mandy nodded.

'Well it doesn't seem like there are any issues,' she told them. 'Liz, you have your own social worker from the mental health team and he's very pleased with how you're doing, so I think the next step is to increase the sleepovers next week to twice a week after today. Then the following week, the boys can stay with you from Friday to Monday. Then, if everyone agrees, they can move back permanently.'

Martin squeezed Liz's hand and they both grinned.

'That works for me,' I smiled.

It was going to be the start of more change. After nearly nine months with me, the twins were going home.

FIVE

Closed Curtains

The kitchen was filled with laughter and chatter, the doors to the garden were open and the table was covered in boxes of takeaway pizza.

We were having a little farewell gathering for Ethan and Albie before they moved back in permanently with their parents the following day. When a child has been with me a while and if it was appropriate, I always liked to mark the occasion and give them a proper goodbye.

Pizza was the twin's favourite food and they were outside with Carol's foster children, Sean, Mary and Dougie, doing their favourite thing – playing football. As well as Carol and her children, my friend and fellow foster carer Vicky had come over, and Louisa and her husband Charlie had called in after work too.

'How are the boys doing?' asked Vicky. 'Are they happy to be going back?'

'They're really happy,' I smiled, watching them kicking the ball around outside. 'They're so excited.'

It was always a satisfying feeling when a child was going back to live with their birth parents and you knew it was the right thing. It helped take away some of the sadness I felt about the boys leaving after being with me for nine months. There had never been any question about Liz or Martin being fit to parent. They'd asked Social Services for help during a difficult time in their lives so there was no animosity there, they were just very grateful. Everyone was pleased to see that Liz was feeling stronger both mentally and physically, and I knew it was in the boys' best interest to be going home.

'Cake time,' I called out to the garden and it was swiftly followed by a stampede of small feet.

I'd picked up a football cake that I'd seen while shopping in Asda.

At the mention of cake, Hannah suddenly appeared too. She'd been watching TV in the living room.

'Hi Hannah,' smiled Louisa. 'How's your new school?'

'OK, I suppose,' she replied.

'Nice kicks,' said Charlie to her.

'Kicks?' I said, puzzled. 'What on earth are those?'

'That's what the youngsters call trainers, Maggie,' laughed Carol.

I looked down at the sparkling white trainers on Hannah's feet. Before I could say anything, she quickly grabbed a piece of cake and went back to the living room.

'Wow, Maggie you're really splashing out on your foster kids these days,' said Charlie.

'What do you mean?' I asked.

'Those Nikes Hannah's wearing cost over £150,' he told me.

'What?' I gasped. 'I wouldn't even spend that on my own shoes, never mind a child's. She must have brought them with her from her mum's house,' I told him.

But as I thought about it, I didn't think I'd ever noticed her wearing them before. They were so gleaming white they looked brand new.

But I didn't have a chance to think any more about it. The rest of the evening passed in a blur of clearing up, getting the boys to bed and packing up the last of their things.

'School in the morning,' I told them as I went to tuck them into their bunk beds for the final time.

'But I thought we were going back to live at Mummy and Daddy's,' said Albie, looking puzzled.

'Don't worry sweetie, you are,' I told him, ruffling his dark hair. 'I'm going to drop you off at school, then your mum and dad will come and pick you up and you will go back and live with them forever. Is that OK?'

They both nodded eagerly.

'I know it's all so exciting but try to get some sleep,' I told them.

As I walked downstairs, it took all my energy to hold back the tears and not dwell on the fact that that would be the last bedtime I would ever do with them.

I went into the living room where Hannah was on her phone. It was still light outside but the curtains were closed.

'Why have you closed the curtains, lovey?' I asked her. 'It's not dark until after nine these days.'

'Oh, I just like it when they're closed, it's nice and cosy,' she said.

'OK,' I shrugged, although I still thought it was a bit odd for a bright June evening.

My eyes were drawn again to the sparkling white trainers on her feet. *Had I seen them before?*

I went into the kitchen and sent Shelley a message asking about the trainers. She responded straight away.

No, I've never bought H any Nikes. Way too £££.

I made two cups of hot chocolate and went back into the living room to sit with her.

'Charlie was right, those really are lovely trainers,' I said casually. 'Where did you get them from?'

'Oh my mum got me them,' she replied, not looking up from her phone.

'That's strange, as I texted your mum and she said she'd never bought you any expensive Nikes before.'

I could see Hannah's face flinch and she knew she'd been rumbled.

'Oh sorry, I forgot – my friend Lizzie got them for me as a present,' she garbled, her cheeks pink.

'Wow, that's very generous,' I replied.

'Her mum works at a sports shop so she gets a massive discount,' she said. 'She gave me them at McDonald's the other week.'

Something wasn't quite adding up but I didn't have any concrete proof that she was lying. For all I knew, Lizzie could have often got stuff for Hannah. I remembered her taking her rucksack with her to McDonald's the other day so if she'd had the trainers inside, I wouldn't have noticed them.

The next morning there was so much to do, trainers were the last thing on my mind. I put the last few things of the twins' into a box and got them their breakfast. As it was their last morning, I made them pancakes.

Our goodbye was going to be at school and I'd deliberately planned it that way to make it very normal and low key. They were so happy about going home, they didn't need to see me sobbing. Just before the bell went, I softly kissed the top of their heads.

'I'm going to miss you both so much, but I know you are going to be so happy being back at home with your mummy and daddy,' I told them.

'You can come and visit us if you want, Maggie,' Ethan said sweetly.

'That's very kind of you lovey,' I told him, swallowing the lump in my throat. 'When you're all settled, I might just take you up on that.'

'You can see our bedroom,' added Albie.

'I can't wait,' I smiled.

As I watched their two little dark heads tearing into their classroom for the very last time, it took all my strength to hold back my tears. I gave them a wave and then the teacher closed the door and that was that.

I managed to hold it together as I walked across the playground. It was only when I was in the safety of my car that the tears started to flow. I knew it was only natural to grieve for what I'd lost. To be honest, the boys had been a joy and my tears were not of sadness. They were lovely kids and they had been easy to look after and fall in love with. But I was so pleased for them, and for Liz and Martin.

Once I'd pulled myself together, I drove round to their flat to drop off the last of their things.

'Come in, Maggie,' Martin smiled.

Their flat was small but immaculately clean and cosy, and they took great pride in showing me the twin's bedroom, which Martin had just redecorated. I'd sent the boys over with the Manchester United duvets and the football rug from my house and Martin had painted the walls a lovely pale blue.

'It looks great,' I told them. 'The boys are going to love sleeping in here.'

I stayed for a cup of tea and a quick chat.

'You know where I am if you need me,' I told them. 'Once the boys have settled, if you ever want a break then just let me know and I'd be happy to have them for an afternoon or even a weekend.'

'That's really kind of you,' smiled Liz.

'Liz has still got her social worker from the mental health team so we've still got lots of support,' Martin told me.

I finished my tea and got up to leave.

'Thank you for everything,' said Liz, looking close to tears.

'My pleasure,' I smiled, giving her a hug. 'Enjoy being a family again.'

I felt a bit teary again as I left the flat but I knew it was the right thing for the boys. In my experience I'd found that, sadly, many children were unable to be returned to their birth families. When a case ended with a happy ending such as this, it was necessary to savour it.

I knew the house was going to feel eerily quiet without Ethan and Albie. Again, I had to make the most of it because the likelihood was it wouldn't last. My agency knew I now had a spare bedroom so I suspected that it wouldn't be long before another child or children needed my help.

But for now, it was just Hannah and I. That night she didn't get in until after seven as it was athletics club and yet again, she texted to say that there was a problem with the bus. She looked absolutely shattered when she walked through the door.

'Why don't you go and have a bath while I sort dinner,' I suggested.

Her school bag was on the side and as it was the end of the week, I decided to put her PE kit in the wash. But when I opened up her bag, to my surprise, the only things in there were a denim mini skirt, a cropped T-shirt and her new Nike trainers. My heart sank and that familiar niggle of doubt churned in my stomach. There was no sign of a PE kit at all.

Hannah's face fell when she came into the kitchen and saw the clothes on the side.

'That's the strangest PE kit I've ever seen,' I told her, my eyebrows raised.

'I've got my kit upstairs,' she replied. 'I had it on under my uniform.'

'What's this then?' I asked her. 'Why did you need to take all this to school?'

'Some of the other girls bring clothes to change into after training so I bought some too but I couldn't be bothered,' she said.

'Well hop upstairs and get your PE kit off so I can put it in the wash,' I told her.

She did so but when she came down, it smelt too freshly washed for clothing she'd just done athletics in. I just couldn't shake the feeling that something was going on here but for every question I had, Hannah always had an answer.

That night, it felt odd just being just the two of us for dinner.

'I wonder how the boys are getting on,' I sighed as I ate a forkful of pasta.

'Am I going to be going back home to my mum's soon?' Hannah suddenly asked.

'I don't honestly know, lovey,' I told her. 'That's something Emma has to decide. The whole idea of you coming into care was to move you away from home as it's not somewhere you can be at the moment,' I told her. 'Plus, you've refused to see your mum and Molly for the past few weeks.'

We were nearly five weeks down the line and I don't think any of us were any clearer about what was going to happen. What I did know was that with regards to Hannah, I hadn't had any problems with her. She wasn't asking to go out at night, she wasn't drinking or smoking, and since the conversation we'd had in her second week, I hadn't had any more reports of her missing classes. She was going to school every day and coming home and doing everything that we'd asked.

'I'm wondering whether this was an issue between Shelley and Hannah rather than anything else,' sighed Emma when she came round for a catch-up one day.

'Maybe the boundaries and the rules weren't tight enough and Hannah took advantage because she could?'

'I don't know,' I sighed. 'I think it's still too soon for us to get a true picture of what's going on. I just don't get that impression from Shelley.'

As the following days passed, I just had a funny feeling that something wasn't right.

Hannah was jumpy and on edge. Every night after she'd got in, I'd find her lingering by the front window, looking out nervously onto the street. Even though they were light early summer nights, she would still always close the curtains at the first available opportunity.

We were having dinner one night and I'd noticed that Hannah was unusually quiet. She sat there anxiously, playing with her food, until she suddenly looked up at me, her blue eyes wide.

'Maggie, if someone types my name into the internet, would they be able to find this address?'

'Well, your address wouldn't be listed anywhere, sweetie, because you're a child, but because I'm a foster carer, Social Services makes sure this address is kept confidential so I don't come up on any internet searches or databases. I don't use my real name on any social media either, so nobody would be able to find out where you're living. Why are you worried about it?'

'No reason,' she said. 'My friend was asking me about fostering and how it works.'

It was an odd thing to ask.

That night I was lying in bed and was just nodding off when something woke me.

Screaming.

I leapt up out of bed and ran down the landing, my heart pounding. It was coming from Hannah's room.

I pushed open her door, my heart in my throat, to find her thrashing around in bed.

'No!' she screamed. 'Don't hurt her! Don't hurt Molly. No!'

She was asleep but she was sobbing and screaming.

I gently shook her awake.

'Hannah, it's OK,' I soothed. 'You're having a bad dream. It's OK.'

Her blue eyes blinked at me in confusion as she slowly started to come round. Her face was soaked in tears and she was sweating. She clung on tightly to my arm and I could feel her whole body shaking.

'Oh flower, it's OK,' I soothed, cuddling her and stroking her tangled blonde hair. 'You were having a bad dream but you're alright.'

She nodded shakily, wiping her eyes.

'What on earth were you dreaming about?' I asked her gently.

'I don't know,' she mumbled.

'Well whatever it was, it was obviously very real,' I told her. 'Do you want to come downstairs and I'll make you a drink?'

She shook her head.

'No, I'm OK,' she told me, lying back down. 'I'm tired. I'm going to go back to sleep.'

I knew I wouldn't be able to sleep after the shock of hearing her blood-curdling screams, so I went down to the kitchen and made a cup of tea. When I went back upstairs, Hannah's light was off.

'Night night,' I told her into the darkness. 'I'm only in my room so shout me if you need me.'

She didn't say anything, and I assumed she'd gone back to sleep.

One afternoon, my supervising social worker Becky came round to see me.

'How are things going with Hannah?' she asked.

'On the face of it, it's going well,' I said. 'I was expecting the worst but she's been absolutely fine. But lately . . .'

My words trailed off.

'But lately what, Maggie?' Becky asked.

'Oh, it's probably nothing,' I replied, embarrassed I'd even brought it up.

But lately there *had* been something.

'Go on, tell me Maggie,' urged Becky. 'Your instincts are normally right. What do you mean?'

All these little niggly things had been eating away at me.

'I don't know,' I sighed. 'I've just got a horrible feeling that something isn't right.'

I explained how Hannah had been jumpy and on edge and I told her about the nightmare.

'It could be the stress of coming into care and starting a new school is just starting to hit her?' suggested Becky.

I shook my head.

'I just feel like it's something else,' I sighed.

My gut instinct was telling me that something was going on behind the scenes. Hannah was hiding something from me and I didn't know what it was yet. But I was as sure as hell going to find out.

SIX

Pieces of the Puzzle

Over the next few days I watched Hannah like a hawk, but on the face of it, everything seemed fine. There were no more nightmares that I was aware of and thankfully I hadn't had any more calls from school about her skipping lessons. Maybe my instincts had been wrong after all. As the days passed, I felt silly that I'd even mentioned it to Becky.

One night when Hannah had gone to bed, I settled down to do some paperwork. I found that I often got more done in the evenings as there were no distractions. But by eleven o'clock, my eyes were stinging with tiredness and I knew it was time to call it a day.

I was just locking up downstairs when my mobile rang. My heart sank and I leapt to answer it. In my experience, it was never good news when someone called you so late.

'Maggie, is Hannah there?' asked a breathless voice. 'Is she OK?'

It was Shelley and she sounded hysterical.

'Yes, she's fine,' I told her, surprised. 'She's upstairs asleep.'

'But is she?' she gasped. 'Please can you go and check that she's OK? Please, Maggie, I'm worried something's happened to her.'

I could hear the desperation in her voice.

'One minute,' I said.

I didn't know what was going on but Shelley had got me worried now. I ran up the stairs with the phone held tight in my hand. Hannah's bedroom door was closed so I gently pushed it open and I poked my head around. Much to my relief, I could see she was in a deep sleep. As the light from the landing filled the room, she murmured and rolled over.

'Shelley, she's fine,' I whispered as I went back downstairs. 'She's in bed fast asleep.'

'Oh thank God,' she sighed. 'I was so worried.'

'But why?' I asked her. 'What's happened?'

Shelley took a deep breath.

'About twenty minutes ago, someone was pounding on the front door. I assumed someone had just got the wrong house and I ignored it as it's so late, but they kept banging and banging, and then they were shouting for Hannah and asking her to come out.'

Panic rose in my throat – that didn't sound good.

'Do you know who it was?' I asked her, concerned.

'I didn't dare look out but it was a male voice,' she said. 'He wouldn't go away and he was getting more and more angry. The next thing I knew, he'd started kicking the door. I was terrified, Maggie. I thought he was going to force his way in. I was about to ring the police but before I got the chance, I heard a car screech off and I realised he must have gone.

'Molly got woken up by all the commotion and looked out of her bedroom window and she saw the car drive off. She couldn't see very well in the dark but she reckons there were three of them in there.'

'Do you think this boy is who she's been hanging around with?' I asked her.

Shelley paused.

'That's what scares me,' she said, her voice cracking. 'It didn't sound like a boy. It was a deep man's voice, Maggie, not a fifteen-year-old boy's.'

It was worrying but as Shelley hadn't actually seen the person at the door, we didn't have any proof that we could act on.

'Maggie, I'm scared,' she said shakily. 'What if these people come looking for Hannah at your house?'

'They won't be able to,' I reassured her. 'They wouldn't know that she was here and my address is protected, so unless Hannah has told them where she's living now, it will be ok.'

But I could tell that Shelley wasn't convinced. We agreed that, even though the men had gone, she should call the police anyway and let them know what had happened.

'I don't suppose there's anything they can do but at least they can log it,' she sighed. 'They know me from all of the times I called them when Hannah didn't come home.'

'Do you want me to talk to Hannah about it in the morning?' I asked her.

'No, no, don't tell her these people were looking for her,' she told me. 'I don't want to worry her or encourage her to get in touch with them again.'

Poor Shelley, I thought as I ended the call. She sounded terrified out of her wits.

As I locked up that night, I felt on edge too.

When it came to Hannah, I felt like I was doing a jigsaw. I had the corner pieces, but I desperately needed the important middle pieces to be able to put the whole puzzle together. It was a case of gathering information bit by bit until I had a true picture of what was going on. After what had happened this evening, it seemed likely that Hannah had a boyfriend and he was part of the group that had been encouraging her to go off the rails. I was guessing he wasn't happy that she'd severed contact with him when she'd come to my house. There was no way that he could know that she was here but it still made me feel uneasy as I bolted the front door.

I thought I'd be too anxious to sleep but I was so exhausted, I must have nodded off. But the next thing I knew, something had jolted me awake.

Was Hannah having a nightmare again? I thought as I sat up in bed. Was that what had woken me?

I couldn't hear anything but I decided to nip to the bathroom to get a drink of water. It was 1 a.m. so I hadn't been asleep for long. All was quiet as I walked along the landing and as I headed back to bed, I decided to look in on Hannah.

Her door was still ajar from when I'd checked on her earlier in the evening when Shelley had phoned. I glanced in and was relieved to see that she was still curled up in bed fast asleep. I was about to go back to my own room when something stopped me.

Call it intuition but something didn't seem right. I looked in at Hannah again. I couldn't see her blonde hair on the pillow or the bed covers moving as she breathed. Somehow it was all too still.

As soon as I got closer to the bed, I knew. My heart was racing as I pulled back the duvet to find Hannah's discarded pyjamas and a sleeping bag I'd had in the wardrobe rolled up to mimic the shape of a body.

She was gone.

I knew she wasn't in the bathroom because I'd just been in there so I quickly turned on the light and ran downstairs to check that she wasn't in the kitchen. But everywhere was eerily quiet. The front door was locked but the bolt and the chain had been taken off. I looked in the drawer in the hall and saw that my house keys were missing.

'Hannah,' I said out loud, feeling sick. 'Where on earth are you?'

And more importantly, who was she with?

The more I thought about it, the more I was convinced that it was the sound of the front door closing that had woken me up.

What the heck was she doing going out at this time of night?

I bolted upstairs, grabbed my mobile and quickly dialled Hannah's number.

Come on, Hannah, answer it, I thought desperately.

My heart sank as I heard the familiar ring tone echoing from the kitchen where her phone was still charging on the worktop.

She'd gone out without it. I quickly typed in the passcode and scrolled through her messages in case it gave me any clues as to who she was with and where she might have gone. But there were just a few jokey, short messages to Lizzie and Martha and some texts from Molly and Shelley. There was nothing incriminating. No strange numbers that she'd texted or rung.

I didn't know what to think anymore, but I felt sick with worry. There was a certain protocol that I had to follow when a child went missing. First, I phoned the out-of-hours social worker at my fostering agency.

'Have you got any idea where she might be?' the woman on the phone asked me.

I told her about the man who had been kicking at Shelley's door earlier that evening.

'I know she was here at eleven o'clock because I checked on her and went to bed shortly afterwards,' I explained.

'As you know, Maggie, because of the time of night I'll need you to report her as a missing person to the police and I'll let the local authority know,' she replied.

'Thanks,' I said.

I rang the police and they took a description of Hannah, including her height, build, hair colour and what she was wearing, which I didn't know. They asked me when I'd last seen her and if I had any idea where she might have gone. I explained that I was her foster carer and I gave them Shelley's name, address and number as they'd have to check that Hannah hadn't gone there.

By the time I'd done all that, I was wide awake. I knew there was no way I was going to be able to sleep while Hannah was missing, so I went upstairs and pulled on a jumper and some jeans so that I wouldn't be in my pyjamas when the police arrived. Then I went down to the kitchen and made myself a cup of tea. I opened the curtains in the living room and stared out into the darkness.

Oh Hannah, where are you and what are you up to? And who on earth are you with?

I was extremely worried. It was now nearly 2 a.m. and she was out wandering the streets.

When my mobile beeped, I grabbed it. It was a text from Shelley.

Just heard from Social Services and police. I'm going out of my mind here. Please text me when H is back. I thought all that was in the past.

I knew there was nothing I could say to stop her worrying.

Of course I will.

All I could do was sit and wait. I turned all the lights off downstairs and sat in the darkness. I didn't want Hannah to get back, see the lights on and know that she'd been rumbled and then run off again. I curled up on the sofa with a blanket and closed my eyes.

I was woken up by the sound of a key in the front door. Or rather, the sound of someone trying to get their key in the door and not doing a very good job of it. I checked the time on my mobile – it was 5 a.m. and just starting to get light. Hannah was obviously hoping to sneak back in before I woke up.

I went to the front door and opened it. Hannah staggered into the hall. She was wearing a short flimsy dress, huge gold hoop earrings and her Nike trainers. Mascara was smudged down her face, red lipstick smeared on her lips and her neck was covered in marks. She looked up at me with heavy blood-shot eyes.

It was clear that she'd been drinking heavily because the smell of alcohol exuded from every pore.

'What on earth's going on, Hannah? I asked her. 'Where have you been?'

'Oh, I jussst needed some freshh air,' she slurred.

'What, for four hours?' I replied. 'I checked your bedroom at one o'clock and you weren't there. It's now five o clock, so where on earth have you been?'

'I'm going to bed now,' she sighed. 'I'm tired.'

She wobbled up the stairs.

I didn't know what to think. I was angry and upset but I knew at this point, I wasn't going to get any sense out of Hannah.

I texted Shelley as I knew she was worried.

Hannah's back. She's OK. I'll ring you in a few hours.

I also rang the police and the out-of-hours social worker to let them know that she was back.

After I'd made my calls, I went upstairs to check on Hannah. She was passed out on her bed, fully clothed.

There was no way that I could sleep now and I wanted to keep an eye on her. I was determined to wake her for school. Then maybe she would realise that it wasn't a good idea to go out in the middle of the night on a school night.

At 7.30 a.m. I tried to wake her.

'Hannah, it's time to get up,' I told her.

'I can't,' she moaned. 'I'm too tired and I feel ill.'

'You should have thought about that when you were sneaking out the door in the early hours of this morning,' I told her firmly.

As I looked down at her though, I knew I was wasting my time. There was no way Hannah was moving, and I couldn't physically force her to get dressed and go in. She was probably still drunk and needed to sleep it off.

I rang the school and got through to Mr Granger, the deputy head of Hannah's year. I explained what had happened.

'I'll do my best to get her to school later on this morning,' I told him.

I got on with some cleaning, looking in occasionally on Hannah, who was still fast asleep. At midday, she wandered sheepishly into the kitchen. She still looked terrible but she'd had a shower and got dressed.

'Why are you in jeans?' I asked. 'Go back upstairs and get your uniform on please, I need to get you to school.'

'But I don't feel well,' she told me hoarsely, her eyes wide.

'You should have thought about that before you left the house at 1 a.m. this morning,' I told her.

Hannah was very meek and did what I'd asked. I drove her there and she didn't say a word.

'I'll see you here at quarter past three,' I told her as we pulled up outside.

'But I can get the bus like I normally do,' she said, looking confused. I shook my head.

'I'm afraid after what happened this morning, I can't trust you to be where you say you are so I'll be picking you up for the foreseeable future,' I told her.

She looked close to tears as she trudged across the road and through the school gates.

I knew I had to be firm with her.

As soon as I got home, I phoned Emma. She already knew what had happened as she'd got an email from the out-of-hours social worker at my agency.

'Is there any indication of where she'd been or who she was with?' she asked.

'Nope, she refused to say anything,' I told her.

'Well at least she's gone to school,' she replied. 'I'll come round after school and talk to her.'

A couple of hours later it was time for me to go and pick Hannah up.

She hardly said a word as she got in the car. It was a good time to try to talk to her as she couldn't go anywhere while I was driving.

'Your mum phoned me last night when you were in bed,' I told her. 'She said someone was knocking at her door last night calling for you. She said it sounded like a man's voice. Were you out with the same person?' I asked. 'Is that your boyfriend?'

I looked in the rear-view mirror and I saw Hannah flinch.

'Can you tell me where you were last night, Hannah?' I asked her again, more gently this time.

She shook her head and tears filled her eyes.

'You need to tell me where you were and who you were with, lovey,' I said again.

'I can't!' she yelled, bursting into tears. 'I just can't. Why do you keep asking me questions? Just leave me alone.'

'Because I'm really worried about you,' I told her, meaning it.

But she wiped her tears and refused to say a single word more.

I knew then that the so-called honeymoon period was well and truly over.

SEVEN

Disappearing Act

Hannah scraped the food around her plate as we sat in silence at the kitchen table.

'Aren't you hungry, lovey?' I asked.

Hannah had hardly said a word throughout the meal. In fact, she'd said very little at all in the days since she'd gone walkabout in the night.

'I'm just tired,' she said, not meeting my eye.

'You're probably still catching up on your sleep after the other night,' I told her.

She ignored me and focused her attention on pushing a sausage and some peas around.

'Hannah, I'm really worried about you,' I told her gently. 'Please tell me what's going on and where you went.'

She shook her head.

'Everyone wants to keep you safe and there's nothing safe about being out on your own in the middle of the night. At least tell me who you were with if you won't tell me what you were doing.'

'I don't want to,' she said, quickly looking away.

But she didn't look away fast enough for me not to notice the tears in her eyes.

What struck me about all this was she wasn't behaving like a typical defiant teenager who was rebelling by going out to drink and have fun. She had a blank look in her eyes and she looked broken.

At least she was being more truthful now. When Emma had questioned her about where she had been, she'd repeatedly told her that she'd been out getting some fresh air.

To be honest, I'd tried to hold back over the past few days and not ask her many questions. I didn't want to give her the third degree because if I did that, I knew there was no way she would ever open up to me. This was currently her home and I didn't want to make it a place of conflict. All I could hope that was as time went by, she'd eventually confide in me about who she was with and what she'd been up to.

Frustratingly, I knew that if she decided to do it again, there was very little that I could do. If Hannah wanted to go out at night again, the reality was that I couldn't stop her. I couldn't physically lock her in her room or stay up all night keeping watch or barricade the front door. The only thing I could do was to lock the door and take my keys and the spare keys up to bed with me. Deep down I knew that this wouldn't stop her going out if she was determined to.

'It's stressful living like this,' I told Vicky when she called one day for a coffee. 'I can't relax, I'm constantly on edge. I wake up in the morning with a sense of dread, wondering if she's going to be there or not. And for the past few days she has, but I don't know how long it's going to last.'

'That's really stressful, Maggie. I can imagine how worried you must be,' sighed Vicky.

I hadn't slept properly since Hannah had last gone missing. Every little creak or noise I would jump awake, convinced it was Hannah trying to get out of the house and I would get up three or four times a night to check on her.

There were dark shadows under my eyes and I was falling asleep in the daytime. I met Graham for lunch one day and I couldn't stop myself from yawning.

'Maggie, are you OK?' he asked, giving my hand a concerned squeeze. 'You look exhausted.'

'I am a bit,' I told him honestly. 'I'm going through a bit of a tricky time with the teenage girl who's living with me at the moment.'

But thankfully, despite my worries, Hannah was always there in the morning. However, I knew I couldn't live like this and I had to start building up trust between us again.

'You can come back from school on the bus today if you want,' I told her casually over breakfast one morning, a couple of weeks after she had gone missing.

'What, you're not coming to pick me up?' she asked, her eyes wide with surprise.

'I thought you might want to get the bus back,' I told her. She looked shocked.

'Really? Can I?'

'Just please make sure you come straight home, Hannah,' I told her wearily.

She nodded eagerly, and I could only hope that I could trust her.

To my relief, she arrived home punctually that afternoon without any issues.

Halfway through the week, Emma had arranged to pop round after school to see Hannah and see how things were going.

Hannah normally got home around 4 p.m., which meant she'd have time to get changed and have a snack before Emma arrived at quarter past. Hannah was still refusing to have any contact with her mum and Molly, and Emma wanted to talk to her about that and see if she might be willing to try to restart things again. I knew Shelley was finding it really hard not seeing her daughter for weeks on end.

I put the kettle on in preparation for Emma's visit and put some biscuits on a plate.

My phone beeped and I expected it to be Emma, telling me that she'd been held up in a meeting or with another case. So I was surprised when I read a text from Martin.

All going well here. Albie and Ethan have settled back brilliantly. We're both so happy to have them home x

It was lovely to know the twins were OK but as I read the text, I also felt a pang of guilt as, with all the worry about Hannah, the twins hadn't been on my mind very much.

When I glanced at the clock, I realised it was 4.10 p.m. and there was no sign of Hannah yet. Much to my relief, a few seconds later there was a knock on the front door.

That will be her, I thought, as she didn't have her own key.

But I was surprised to find Emma standing there.

'Sorry I'm a bit early,' she smiled. 'For once the traffic was OK.'

Emma must have seen the look of confusion on my face.

'What is it, Maggie?' she asked, concerned. 'What's happened?'

'Oh it's just Hannah's not home from school yet,' I told her. 'The bus must be running late or something. I'm sure she'll be back any minute.'

But I knew what we were both thinking.

I quickly grabbed my phone and sent her a text.

Emma is here. Are you on your way?

But there was no response. I went into the living room and tried ringing her. It went straight to voicemail so I left a message.

By four thirty there was still no sign of her and I could see Emma glancing anxiously at the clock.

By five o'clock she was pacing the kitchen floor.

'I'm sorry to leave you with this, Maggie, but I'm going to have to go back to the office now,' she said. 'I can't wait any longer.'

'I understand,' I replied.

'Keep in touch though and let me or the out-of-hours team know if you think she's done one of her disappearing acts again.'

'I will do,' I sighed wearily, already dreading the long night of worry I might have ahead of me.

When Emma had gone, I rang Hannah's school just to check she wasn't still there. Someone in the office answered and said there was no one left in the building but the teachers. Then I called my agency and managed to catch Becky before she left the office.

'Oh no, not again, Maggie,' she sighed. 'Let's give her until 10 p.m. and if she's not back by then phone the police and report her as missing.'

I had déjà vu as I sat in the living room and waited. I turned on the TV but I wasn't really watching it. All I could think about was Hannah and where on earth she was.

Time dragged. I couldn't face cooking a proper meal, so I made myself a sandwich but I couldn't eat it because I felt sick with worry. I knew there was no way I could go to bed until Hannah came back. That was if she *did* come back.

Then, just before ten, I saw a figure stagger past the front window and up the path. It was followed by loud banging on the door.

She was back. But what kind of a state was she in?

My stomach churned with dread as I opened the front door to find Hannah slumped there. She was still wearing her school uniform and her bare legs were covered in bruises.

She giggled and fell through the doorway.

'Where on earth have you been?' I asked her.

She just made a strange moaning noise and I put my arms around her shoulders.

'Hannah, look at me,' I told her.

I tilted her face towards mine. Her pupils were dilated and her eyes rolled back into her head.

'Do you know where you are?' I asked her.

She tried to speak but gibberish came out and her head lolled forward. My instincts told me that this wasn't drink, it was something else.

'Hannah, what have you taken?' I asked her but she couldn't speak.

I quickly phoned the out-of-hours social worker at my fostering agency and explained the situation.

'She's obviously had some sort of drug and she's completely out of it,' I told her.

'I think you need to get her to hospital, Maggie,' she told me. 'It's just a precaution, but we don't know what she's taken or how much of it she's had and we just can't risk it.'

I knew she was right. I couldn't risk putting Hannah to bed in this state.

It took all of my efforts to get her into the car. She could barely walk and I practically had to drag her. I lowered her into the front seat and she slumped there, lifeless.

'Talk to me, Hannah,' I urged as I drove along. 'Are you OK?'

All she did was utter a moan.

I managed to find a parking space near the entrance to the hospital and then I put my arm around her waist and led her to Accident and Emergency. I left her slumped on a plastic chair while I registered her at the front desk.

'I'm afraid it's going to be a bit of wait,' the receptionist told me. 'We're extremely busy tonight.'

I tried to keep Hannah awake but she was talking gibberish and was slumped over. It was terrifying seeing the vacant, blank look in her glazed eyes.

We sat there for two hours until eventually a nurse came out and called Hannah's name and took us into a cubicle.

'What's your name, darling?' she asked her.

Hannah just moaned.

'Can you tell me how old you are?' she asked her.

Hannah shook her head and her eyes rolled back into her head.

'Do you know what she's taken?' she asked me and I had to confess that I had no idea.

I explained what had happened, that Hannah was in care and I was her foster carer.

'She seems OK. Her breathing's not compromised and her heart rate's slightly accelerated but nothing to worry about. I don't think she's overdosed. I expect from looking at her that she's taken something like ketamine but it's hard to know without testing her urine and even then it might not show up,' she told me. 'What I'd like to do is keep her in here for the next few hours so we can keep an eye on her and make sure she drinks plenty of fluids.'

'OK,' I said.

It was now after midnight and I knew it was going to be a long night ahead of us.

Hannah was quiet now and she looked like she was asleep, so I took the opportunity to nip out and quickly let my agency know what was happening. They said they would email Emma and update her. She would probably contact Shelley in the morning.

When I came back in, Hannah was stirring. She moaned and tossed and turned. Her eyelids flickered and she winced as she opened them.

'It's so bright in here,' she sighed. 'Where am I? What are you doing to me?'

There was no point asking her any questions; I could see she was still as high as a kite. All I could do was sit with her and wait for the effects to wear off.

Hannah dozed on and off but I could tell that she wasn't in a deep sleep. Her forehead was wet with sweat and she tossed and turned. Occasionally she moaned or cried out something that I couldn't understand.

I sat in a chair next to her bed, my eyes heavy with tiredness, but there was no way I was going to get any sleep; I
was too busy watching Hannah like a hawk.

At 7 a.m. the nurse came to check on Hannah.

'She seems OK,' she told me. 'I think she just needs to go
home now and sleep it off.'

Hannah moaned and opened her eyes.

'My head really hurts,' she croaked.

'It will do, sweetheart,' the nurse told her. 'You're coming
down from whatever you took last night.

'What did you take?' she asked her.

Hannah closed her eyes and looked embarrassed. 'I don't
know,' she sighed.

She was still very weak and wobbly but I managed to help
her out of bed and take her to the toilet. It was gone eight
by the time we walked out of the hospital.

'Do I have to go to school?' asked Hannah, blinking in the
early morning sunshine.

'I don't think you're in any fit state after last night,' I told
her. 'I think you just need to go home and sleep this off.'

I knew there was no point in asking her any questions.
What we both needed to do was sleep. We drove home in
silence, Hannah resting her head on the window with her
eyes closed.

When we got home, she got changed into her pyjamas
while I phoned her school. I spoke to Mr Granger and
explained what had happened.

'I hope she's OK,' he told me.

'She will be,' I said.

When I went upstairs to check on her, Hannah was lying

on her bed. I thought she was already asleep but as I closed her door, she mumbled, 'I'm sorry, Maggie.'

I was sorry too. Sorry that she felt the need to get into this state. Sorry that she was making the wrong choices and putting herself at risk like that.

And, just like Shelley had been, I felt angry with frustration that I was unable to stop her. Where was this going to end? When Hannah failed to come home at all one night? When she overdosed on drugs or did something silly when she was drunk?

She needed to start talking to me about what was really going on. Because until then, nobody was going to be able to help her.

EIGHT

Rock Bottom

'It's happened again,' I sighed wearily down the phone to Emma as I sat in my car.

It had been three days since Hannah had failed to come home after school and I'd had to take her to hospital. Now she had disappeared again and it was soul-destroying.

Tonight she'd had athletics so she'd told me to collect her at school at 6 p.m.

'It will be easier if I meet you there rather than you trying to find the stadium where we train,' she'd said.

So at six o'clock, I'd pulled up outside school and waited and waited. After twenty minutes, there was still no sign of Hannah, or any other pupil for that matter. I'd texted and called her mobile but there had been no reply and it had gone straight to voicemail.

Eventually I'd buzzed on the intercom at the school gates. Luckily there were a few teachers still left in the building so one of them had let me in.

'I'm here to collect Hannah Dougan,' I'd told him.

I'd explained that she'd had athletics club but that she'd told me to pick her up at school.

'She told me to meet her here rather than trying to find the stadium,' I'd explained. 'And it's raining so I thought she might have waited inside.'

'Well I'm a PE teacher here and we don't use a stadium,' he'd told me, puzzled. 'We did have an athletics club, but the teacher who ran it is off sick so it hasn't been on for the past six weeks or so. As far as I know, Hannah never came along when it was running.'

'But for the past couple of months, Hannah's been doing athletics after school on a Tuesday and Thursday,' I'd said.

He'd shaken his head.

'Not here, she hasn't,' he'd replied.

That was the moment that I'd realised I'd been well and truly conned. Twice a week Hannah had been getting in at seven o'clock, and if she hadn't been at athletics club then where on earth had she been going once school had finished? What had she been doing for those four hours, and who had she been with?

'I don't know what to believe anymore,' I told Emma as I sat in the car outside school. 'I feel like the wool has been well and truly pulled over my eyes.'

'I'm with you, Maggie,' she sighed. 'I don't think any of us know what's really going on with Hannah.'

Unfortunately, this was becoming such a regular occurrence by now that I knew the drill.

'I'll head home and if she's not back by ten, then I'll call the police,' I told Emma.

'Well hopefully it won't come to that,' she replied. 'But

keep in touch with out-of-hours and they'll keep me updated. I hope she comes back soon, Maggie.'

'Me too,' I sighed.

I drove home with a heavy heart. I was so angry and frustrated with Hannah, but I couldn't stop myself from worrying either. Of course I wanted her to come back but I was also dreading it – what kind of state she was going to be in? Was she going to be drunk or high on drugs? Was tonight going to involve another trip to the hospital? It didn't bear thinking about.

As is always the case when you're watching the clock, time dragged. I tried to eat some of the casserole I'd made for dinner but I wasn't hungry. I put the TV on but I couldn't concentrate. All I could think about was Hannah. Even though I knew I hadn't done anything wrong to cause this, I felt a huge sense of responsibility. This child was living in my house and she had gone missing yet again. It was hard not to blame myself.

I'd convinced myself that she would probably turn up around ten, as that was the time that she had come back the other evening. But when ten o'clock came and went, I felt sick to my stomach.

I went up to my bedroom, sat on my bed and stared out of the window onto the street below. It was dark outside now and everything seemed much more menacing in the darkness. It was also still pouring with rain and even though it was June, I could hear the wind rattling outside. I sighed heavily and picked up my phone, ready to put the wheels in motion. I called my agency and then the police to report Hannah as a missing person. I knew the exact information that they needed – a physical description, where she was last seen and I was told an officer would come round to see me in person.

'Please call us if she comes back in the meantime,' the operator told me.

'I will do,' I replied.

When my phone rang, I leapt on it, but my heart sank as I saw Vicky's name flashing up on the screen.

'Sorry to call you so late, Maggie,' she said, her tone light. 'I just wondered if I could pop by tomorrow morning and borrow your cake tin? I want to make a birthday cake for one of my kids and I've just realised my tin has gone walkabout.'

'Oh, er, yes of course you can,' I replied.

But she must have sensed there was something wrong by the tone of my voice.

'Is everything OK, Maggie?' she asked. 'You sound very flat.'

'Hannah's gone missing again,' I sighed. 'I've just called it in and I'm waiting for the police to arrive.'

'Oh, I'm so sorry,' she said sympathetically. 'She really is giving you the runaround. 'You just can't rest until they're back, can you?'

Vicky was right, of course.

Eleven o'clock rolled around and there was still no news. I knew there was no point getting ready for bed as I might have to go out again. This was becoming all too familiar, I thought as I lay in the darkness in the eerily quiet house.

My mind was whirring. I couldn't give up on Hannah – that wasn't in my nature – but I could see how exhausting, both physically and emotionally, this must have been for Shelley and Molly, not knowing if and when she'd be back. Hannah had to start talking to us.

She had to – before something serious happened.

At midnight, there was a loud knock on the door. I jumped up and raced into the hall.

'Where on earth have you been?' I muttered as I undid the bolt.

I held my breath as I hurriedly opened the door, but to my dismay, it wasn't Hannah at all. Instead, two female police officers were standing on the doorstep. One was tall and blonde and very young, while the other lady had dark hair and was quite a bit older than her colleague. The two PCs introduced themselves and then proceeded to search the house – something I knew that they had to do as part of the procedure when a child was missing. They had to check that Hannah wasn't actually hiding somewhere and I hadn't noticed. Thankfully they were both really calm and understanding.

'My sister's a foster carer,' the older PC with the dark hair told me kindly. 'I can't imagine doing what you do.'

Once they'd finished searching all the rooms, I went through Hannah's description with them again and they asked why she might have gone missing. I explained her history and why she'd come into the care system.

'Do you know anyone she might be with?' the older PC asked. 'Could she have gone to her mum's house?'

'I doubt it,' I sighed. 'She's refused to see her mother for a number of weeks.'

But I knew as a process of elimination they would have to contact Shelley and double-check that she wasn't there.

In the meantime they'd log Hannah on the system to say that she was missing and issue her description and a photograph that I'd given them.

'Try not to worry – I'm sure she'll turn up,' the older PC told me.

My worry was that even if she did, there was no telling what kind of a state she was going to be in.

After they'd gone, I made a cup of tea. A long night of waiting loomed ahead so I sat back down on the sofa and closed my eyes.

Come on Hannah, I willed. *Where are you?*

I cried out as I bolted upright to a clattering sound. Light streamed into the living room and I heard the crash of a bin lorry outside. I sat up in a panic.

It was 7.30 a.m.

My stomach sank as the realisation hit me.

Hannah hadn't come back. She was still missing.

I felt so guilty that I'd still managed to fall asleep.

I frantically checked my phone but I hadn't had any missed calls or texts. I felt an impending sense of doom that something awful had happened to her. This was the longest that she'd been missing while she was living with me and she'd never disappeared overnight before. I'd assumed she would have turned up by now and I was desperately worried that something was terribly wrong. I tried her mobile again but like last night, it went straight to voicemail.

Just after eight thirty, Becky rang.

'How are you doing, Maggie?' she asked. 'Any updates?'

'Nothing,' I sighed. 'She hasn't turned up and there hasn't been any word from the police.'

When my phone rang again a little later, I leapt on it. It was Mr Granger from Hannah's school.

'I thought I'd better let you know that Hannah's not turned up today,' he told me.

'I'm so sorry,' I told him. 'I completely forgot to ring you.'

I explained what had happened.

'I hope she turns up soon,' he said. 'Keep us posted.'

'I will do,' I replied.

It was a waiting game and it was so frustrating. I didn't know what to do with myself. All I could do was try to carry on as normal and make sure my phone was by my side.

In a bid to wake myself up, I had a very quick shower. All the time I had one ear out for the front door in case Hannah came back.

Just after 11 a.m. I heard my phone ringing in the kitchen. I ran down and got to it just in time. It was an unregistered number.

'Is that Mrs Hartley?' a man's voice asked.

'Yes,' I said, too worried about what they were going to say to correct them and tell them I was a Miss.

He explained that he was a police officer in a town about an hour and half's drive from me.

'Did you report a Hannah Dougan missing?' he asked.

My heart was pounding out of my chest.

'Yes,' I said nervously. 'Have you found her?'

'We have,' he replied. 'She was picked up on some land out in the countryside.'

My head spun as I tried to take it all in.

'Is she OK?' I asked. 'Where is she now?'

'She's in an ambulance on the way to the local hospital,' he told me. 'We need to get her checked over. She's been out in the rain overnight so she's very cold and wet.'

There was no time to ask any more questions.

'I'll get in the car now and meet you there,' I told him. 'I need to phone Hannah's social worker too as I'm sure she'll want to come along.'

I sprung into action. I jumped in my car and looked up the name of the hospital where they were taking her on my sat nav. My mind was in overdrive. What the hell was she doing in the countryside so far away from here? Had she been drinking or taking drugs? Was she badly hurt?

I quickly called Emma.

'I've just heard from the police,' I told her. 'They've got her.'

'Thank goodness,' she sighed.

I gave her the details of the hospital.

'I'll meet you there, Maggie, and I'll give Shelley a call too,' she replied.

I couldn't get to the hospital quick enough. It felt like it was taking forever as I tried to find a space to park and then queued up for a ticket. I dashed across the car park towards the signs for Accident and Emergency.

I ran up to the front desk and gave them Hannah's name.

'The police were bringing her in and I said I would meet them here,' I panted, feeling frantic.

'And you are?' asked the receptionist.

'I'm her foster carer,' I told her, showing her my official ID. 'She's in the care system. Her social worker's on her way but she's not going to be here for a while.'

The woman tapped away at her computer while I drummed my fingers impatiently on the desk.

'She's in bay six down the corridor,' she told me eventually, pointing to a doorway.

My stomach churned as I dashed down the corridor trying to see the numbers on the cubicles either side of me. I was desperate to see Hannah but equally I dreaded what I was going to find. At long last, I got to bay six and nervously pulled the blue curtain to one side.

Hannah was lying on top of the bed with two police officers sat on chairs either side of her. I took one look at her and my mouth gaped open in horror.

'Oh lovey,' I gasped, tears filling my eyes. 'What on earth has happened to you?'

She was filthy and covered in mud. Her hair was all matted and wet, and despite the make-up streaked down her face, I could see she had a black eye. She was wearing a flimsy red dress that I'd never seen before, but one strap had snapped and the bottom was all ripped. Her legs were covered in cuts and bruises and she only had one shoe on.

She looked up at me, her big blue eyes filled with pure fear, and any anger that I'd felt melted away.

'You poor, poor girl,' I soothed, stroking her damp, matted hair. 'Who did this to you, lovey?'

She didn't say anything. She clutched a hospital blanket around her shoulders but I could see that she was trembling.

'You must be Hannah's foster carer?' one of the male PCs asked.

'Yes, I'm Maggie,' I told him. 'And Hannah's social worker is on her way too.'

'I'm PC Davis,' said one of them, standing up. 'And this is my colleague PC Henry. We wanted to stay with her until you arrived.'

'Thank you,' I said.

'Can we step outside and have a quick word?' he asked.

'I'm just going to pop out and have a chat with the police officers,' I told Hannah gently.

'Are you coming back?' she whispered.

Her eyes were so puffy and red that she could barely see out of them.

'Of course I am, flower,' I said, squeezing her hand. 'I'll only be a few minutes.'

I stood in the corridor with the police officers. They were both huge, tall blokes in their thirties.

'Where on earth did you find her?' I asked them, breathlessly.

'We had a call this morning from a gentleman who owns a house in a nearby village,' PC Davis told me. 'He says he heard a car screech up about midnight last night when he and his wife were in bed. He said he looked out of his window and saw somebody push something out of the back seat of a car onto his land. Apparently he's had recurring problems with fly-tipping so he assumed it was someone dumping a bag of rubbish. It was only when he took his dog for a walk this morning that he saw it wasn't a bag of rubbish, it was a young girl. He found her curled up, passed out on the wet grass,' he said. 'He called 999 straight away.'

Tears pricked my eyes as I thought of Hannah being dumped out of a car in the middle of nowhere like a bag of rubbish. What kind of a person would do that to a child?

As we talked, a man in green scrubs walked over to us.

'Here's the doctor now,' said PC Davis.

'I'm Hannah's foster carer,' I told him, introducing myself. 'How is she?'

'She's dehydrated and cold from being out in the rain overnight,' he told me. 'She's a bit battered and bruised, but it's mainly shock and trauma.'

He went to check on Hannah while I stayed outside with the police.

'She's very lucky as the temperature can really drop out there on the hills, but thankfully it was a fairly mild night,' PC Davis told me. 'We suspect she's been drinking too. She was very unsteady and disorientated but she managed to tell us her name. When we searched the database it alerted us to your missing persons report. Has she done this before?'

I nodded my head sadly.

'She's disappeared before, but never overnight like this. Who on earth did this to her?' I asked.

PC Davis shrugged.

'She won't say a word,' he sighed. 'All she would tell us was that she'd been to a party.'

'A party?' I gasped.

What kind of party was it where you ended the night battered and bruised, being pushed out of car and abandoned in the middle of nowhere miles from home?

'She's in too much shock to make a statement, but when she's feeling stronger, we'd like to go through everything with her,' PC Davis told me, handing me his details. 'We want to know who has done this to her.'

'Me too,' I sighed. 'Me too.'

As the police officers left, I saw Emma heading down the corridor towards me, a grim look on her face.

'How is she?' she asked as she'd reached me.

'Have a look for yourself,' I sighed.

We both went back into the cubicle and Emma had the same horrified reaction that I'd had.

'Oh, Hannah,' she gasped. 'This has got to stop.'

'It's never going to stop,' Hannah said, her voice cracking.

'What do you mean, sweetie?' I asked her.

A tear rolled down her bruised face and she refused to say any more.

I could see now that this was far more serious than a girl going off the rails. It was something much more sinister.

Emma went out to talk to the doctor while I sat with Hannah. I sat and held her hand in a bid to comfort her and reassure her that she was safe. She didn't say a word and I could see her eyes were flickering with exhaustion. By the time Emma came back in, she'd fallen into a deep sleep.

'Maggie, why don't you go home and get Hannah a few things?' she suggested, keeping her voice low. 'I think they're going to keep her in overnight for observation tonight just as a precaution. I'm happy to stay with her for now and you need a break. You look exhausted.'

'OK,' I nodded, 'but I want to come back later.'

I hated leaving Hannah when she was in such a state but Emma was right. I could barely keep my eyes open and I took some comfort in the fact that Hannah was safe and not alone.

As I walked out, PC Davis was still in reception.

'I was just coming to find you,' he told me. 'I forgot to mention that Hannah had a bag with her when she was found.'

He handed me her school bag, which was just as muddy as the rest of her clothes.

'Thank you,' I told him. 'I'll take it home with me for safe keeping.'

'Hopefully her scare last night will teach her to keep out of trouble,' he told me. 'They're obviously not a nice crowd she's been hanging around with, so hopefully this will be the lesson that she needs to keep away from them. We can press charges, but only if Hannah gives a statement and tells us what happened to her last night.'

'I hope so too. I'll talk to her.'

When I got home, I didn't know what to do first. I went up to Hannah's bedroom and packed some pyjamas, her tooth-brush, a book and a change of clothes to take to the hospital. At the last minute, I also picked up the stuffed mouse Shelley had put in for her. Then I looked at her muddy school bag.

I'll empty it out and try and give it a clean down, I thought.

I unzipped the rucksack. Stuffed in the top was her school uniform and PE kit.

So much for athletics club, I sighed, taking out the clothes and putting them in the laundry basket.

To my surprise, at the bottom of the bag there was a blue lunch box. I was puzzled. I didn't recognise it and Hannah always had school dinners.

Intrigued, I unclipped it and looked inside, expecting to find all sorts of mouldy, rotten food. Instead, there was a large package covered in cling film. I tried to open it but it was tightly wrapped with layer upon layer of sticky plastic film. At last I managed to break into it. When I finally ripped off the last layer, I stared in horror at what I'd found.

'What the . . .?' I gasped.

It wasn't a sandwich. There was a large roll of notes with an elastic band around them and three small bags of white powder.

What on earth had Hannah got herself into?

NINE

Hidden Secrets

My heart was pounding as I undid the elastic band and counted out the rolled-up money. I was shocked to find there was over £300 in £20 and £50 notes. What on earth was Hannah doing with that kind of money stuffed in her school bag?

But it wasn't the cash that terrified me the most. It was the three small, plastic bags wrapped in the cling film parcel along with the cash. Each of them was filled with white powder and knotted at the top. It didn't take a genius to hazard a guess at what they were and I didn't even dare touch them. I knew I needed to ring my agency straight away and report this. My hands were shaking as I dialled Becky's number.

As soon as she answered, I described what I'd found.

'Oh my God, Maggie,' Becky gasped. 'What on earth has this girl got herself into?'

'I honestly don't know,' I sighed. 'But I want these things out of my house as soon as possible. What should I do?'

'I'll call Emma and tell her what's happened,' said Becky. 'You need to contact the police.'

'But what's going to happen to Hannah if I do that?' I asked worriedly.

'I don't know,' replied Becky. 'But with something as serious as this we've got to go through the official channels. This has gone beyond Social Services and is far too big for us to handle on our own.'

I knew she was right. I was utterly unnerved by what I'd found and I wanted the cash and what I strongly suspected were drugs out of my house. If I rang the police, I knew it might be hours before they came round. I made my mind up.

Carefully placing the cash and the bags of white powder back into the lunch box, I stuffed it into my handbag, grabbed the bag I'd packed for Hannah and drove to the local police station.

I parked as close as I could to the main entrance, but even as I walked down the high street with my handbag pressed close to my chest, I felt sick. I felt as though every passer-by knew exactly what I had in my bag and that at any minute, someone was going to tap on my shoulder.

At the police station my stomach churned with nerves as I approached the woman on the front desk. There were a few people sitting in the waiting room and I felt very conscious about them overhearing what I was about to say. I put my bag on the counter and as quietly as I could, explained that I was a foster carer.

'This afternoon I was going through one of my young people's school bags as she's in hospital at the moment and I came across this,' I told her, keeping my voice low.

I opened up the lunch box and showed her the roll of notes and the white powder.

'Oh right, I see,' she said, clearly surprised. 'Let me get one of my colleagues to take you through to an interview room and get a few more details.'

I took a seat in the waiting room, still feeling incredibly conspicuous.

I knew I was naïve when it came to drugs and my knowledge of them was limited. I'd found drugs in foster children's bedrooms before but that had been years ago. One teenage boy had hidden a small bag of marijuana in a drawer that I'd stumbled across whilst putting his socks away, and I'd also found what turned out to be an acid tab in the trouser pocket of another teenager I was fostering. In those days, my area had a police officer who would patrol locally and I'd got to know him well over the years. When I'd discovered the drugs, I'd told the PC what I'd found and he'd given the young people involved a stern talking to and I'd never had an issue again after that. Now, thanks to police cuts, my local bobby on the beat was long gone and I'd also never dealt with anything on this scale before, which was why it was so terrifying. Did these drugs belong to Hannah? I knew she had taken drugs before, but I'd never suspected that she was an addict. Now I wasn't so sure.

'Ms Hartley?' asked a voice.

I looked up to see a blonde-haired police officer standing there.

'I'm PC Williams,' she said. 'Do you want to come through?'

I clutched my bag tightly to my chest and gave her a weak smile.

'Thank you,' I replied nervously.

She led me through a door, down a corridor and into a small, windowless interview room.

'So what can we help you with today?' she asked.

I explained what had happened before taking out the roll of money and the packages of white powder and placing them on the table.

'I don't know for sure what it is,' I finished. 'It might be nothing but it looks like drugs to me.'

'I think you're right,' she nodded.

She asked me question after question about Hannah and why she was in my care, her behaviour over the past few months and who she had been hanging around with. I answered as best as I could while she took notes.

'There's a lot I can't tell you,' I explained. 'Because I just don't know myself.'

She nodded and took some notes and I gave her my number and Emma's contact details.

'What will happen now?' I asked her.

'I strongly suspect that tests will show that this is a class A drug – probably cocaine,' PC Williams told me. 'It's a lot of cocaine and cash for a fifteen-year-old girl to be carrying around in her bag. So rather than just possession, we're probably looking at the fact that she has been supplying it to people.'

I felt sick to my stomach. Surely Hannah wasn't a drug dealer?

'Of course, these are very serious allegations, so we need to interview Hannah about them as soon as we can,' she told me.

'But she's in hospital at the moment,' I replied. 'I'm about to drive there now and see her.'

'We'll wait to speak to her, depending on her condition,' PC Williams told me. 'Why is she in hospital?'

I explained everything that had taken place over the last twenty-four hours.

'She's obviously very traumatised, but they're mainly keeping her in overnight for observation,' I added.

'OK,' she said. 'What I need you and her social worker to do is keep in touch with us. When she's discharged tomorrow, we'll need someone to bring her here to the station to be questioned. Obviously she will need an appropriate adult with her too.

'But if things change and she's not discharged tomorrow then I'm afraid we will need to go up to the hospital and talk to her,' she added. 'These are serious allegations and there can't be too much of a delay in her being interviewed.'

'OK,' I nodded. 'But what shall I say to Hannah? Do I tell her that I found the stuff in her bag?'

I couldn't even begin to imagine how to have that conversation with Hannah, and I dreaded to think how she might respond.

'Please don't say anything at all to her at this stage,' PC Williams told me firmly. 'If she knows what you've found and that the police want to speak to her then there's a real risk that she might abscond and that's the last thing we all want to happen.'

'But how on earth am I going to get her to the police station without letting her know what's happening?' I asked, perplexed.

'Tell her at the last possible moment when you're on your way here,' she advised.

I had no idea how I was going to go back to the hospital and act as though nothing had happened when, in reality, I had a million and one questions rushing around my head. Where had the drugs come from? How long had she been involved in this mess?

I wanted nothing more than to sit Hannah down and ask her what on earth she had been up to. But deep down I knew that what PC Williams was saying was for the best.

'Do you think Hannah is in danger?' I asked her.

She shrugged sadly.

'Drugs are a dangerous game,' she sighed. 'Anyone involved in taking them, making them or dealing in them is always going to be at risk.'

I'd been so naïve. I thought Hannah had got in with the wrong crowd and had been out drinking and partying. Never in a million years had I suspected that she was involved in drug dealing.

I walked out of the police station with a heart heavy with worry about what on earth was going to happen to Hannah. I checked my phone and realised I had three missed calls from Emma. I rang her straight back.

'Maggie, what on earth is going on?' she gasped. 'Becky rang and told me about what you'd found in Hannah's school bag.'

'I know,' I sighed. 'It's unbelievable. God only knows what she has got herself into.'

I explained that I'd handed the money and the drugs into the police station.

'They want to interview Hannah.'

'Right now?' she asked.

'They want us to bring her down to the station as soon as she's discharged, assuming that's tomorrow morning. Otherwise they want to interview her at the hospital. But they don't want us to say anything in case she runs off.'

Emma told me she'd left the hospital and was back in the office, but she reassured me that Hannah was doing OK.

'I left when Shelley arrived,' she told me. 'She was very upset about what had happened but relieved that she was OK and had been found.'

'Should we tell Shelley about the drugs and what's happened with the police?' I asked.

'I don't want to worry her or risk her saying anything to Hannah, so let's wait until tomorrow when we're on our way to the station,' Emma told me.

It was well after five o'clock by the time I'd driven the hour and a half back to the hospital. As I was walking down the corridor, I bumped into one of the nurses who had come in to check on Hannah earlier when I'd been sitting with her.

'How's Hannah doing?' I asked her.

'She's mainly been sleeping,' she told me. 'We've got some fluids into her and she's even had something to eat. We're going to move her to a ward shortly and all being well, she should be able to go home in the morning.'

'That's a relief,' I sighed.

'She did get quite anxious and upset earlier because she was worried that she'd lost her school bag,' added the nurse. 'She said she'd had it with her?'

I nodded.

'I've got it safely at home. I'll let her know.'

It was no wonder that she was worried about her bag with everything that was inside it.

I hesitated outside Hannah's cubicle. It felt strange seeing her and not being able to say anything about what I'd found. There were so many questions I wanted to ask her but for now, they would have to wait.

I pulled back the curtain and walked in. Hannah was fast asleep so I sat on the chair beside her bed. She was wearing a hospital gown instead of the ripped red dress and her face had been cleaned up, but it was still puffy and swollen and her eye had turned from blue to black. She looked tiny lying there in the bed, and I couldn't match this image of a young girl with the piles of cash and drugs I'd discovered.

Oh Hannah, I thought. What's going on? What have you got yourself into?

She was only fifteen. Up until a few months ago she'd been an ordinary schoolgirl. I was absolutely convinced someone must have put her up to this, but I couldn't begin to imagine who it might be.

I sat quietly, mulling it all over in my mind. After ten minutes or so, Hannah started to stir. She tossed and turned and then sat up with a start.

'Are you OK, lovey?' I asked her gently.

She blinked in confusion.

'Where is it, Maggie?' she asked frantically, her eyes wide. 'Do you know where my bag is?'

'Oh, the police gave it to me so I took it home,' I told her casually. 'Don't worry, I put it in your room where it's safe.'

She collapsed back onto the pillows, a look of relief on her face.

I spent the next couple of hours by Hannah's bedside while she dozed on and off.

'I'm going to head home now and let you get some rest,' I told her gently. 'But hopefully you're going to be discharged in the morning so Emma and I will come and collect you.'

She nodded, looking dazed.

'I hope you manage to get some more sleep,' I added, stroking her forehead.

I still felt guilty that I was keeping the fact that I had gone to the police from her. Even if it was in her best interests, I knew Hannah would feel that I had betrayed her trust.

When I got home, I rang Vicky for a chat. As she was a foster carer too, I knew that she would keep things confidential, and it was a relief to be able to talk to someone about what had happened.

'Oh my goodness,' she gasped when I'd finished. 'I never would have thought that Hannah would be into anything like that.'

'She's very good at keeping secrets. But I do feel awful,' I sighed. 'Like I've betrayed her.'

'You're just doing your job, Maggie,' she told me. 'As foster carers our role is to protect kids and by going to the police, that's what you're doing.'

'I know Hannah's not going to see it like that, though,' I sighed. 'And what on earth's going to happen to her being caught in possession of such a large quantity of drugs?'

'At the end of the day, you did what you had to,' Vicky reassured me. 'It's in the police's hands now.'

The next morning I woke up with an impending sense of doom about the day ahead. I was dreading having to tell Hannah we were taking her to the police station to be questioned. I honestly didn't know how she was going to react but I imagined she would be scared and angry.

Emma and I had arranged to meet at the hospital in the morning before telling Hannah.

'It's better to have two of us here just in case she tries anything,' Emma reiterated as we walked across the car park towards the hospital entrance.

'Are we going to tell her now, or wait until we're on the way?' I asked.

Emma hesitated.

'We've both got our cars with us and if we wait until we're on the way, one of us will have to tell her on their own,' she said. 'And I don't want to tell her right at the last minute because she'll have realised by then that we're not going to your house. I also don't want to be taking her in for questioning if she's hysterical. I think we need to tell her here at the hospital to at least give her a chance to try to process it.'

'I'm happy to follow your lead,' I told her. I felt sick at the thought of what we were about to do, but I knew there was going to be no easy way of breaking this news.

Hannah had been moved to the ward and when we arrived, she was sitting on the bed, dressed and ready to go. She still looked very pale and frail, but she'd had a shower and changed into some clothes that I'd brought her the previous day.

'How are you feeling, lovey?' I asked her.

'OK,' she shrugged, fiddling with the blanket and not meeting my eye.

'Well the doctor said you're well enough to be discharged, which is good news,' Emma told her.

'Great,' she said, getting up. 'Shall we go then?'

Emma and I exchanged glances and Hannah looked at Emma suspiciously as she pulled the curtains around the bed.

'I think you'd better sit down for a minute, Hannah,' she told her.

'But why? I thought we were going?' she asked, looking concerned.

'We are, lovey,' I said. 'But there's something Emma needs to talk to you about first.'

My heart started racing. As Emma began to speak, I couldn't look at Hannah.

'When the police found you yesterday morning, they also found your school bag,' she explained. 'So they gave it to Maggie for safe keeping to take home. When she took it home, she opened it to give it a cleanout as it was covered in mud—'

'No!' yelled Hannah. 'Why would you do that, Maggie? That's *my* bag and it's none of your business.'

I felt tears choking in my throat as I saw the distress in Hannah's eyes. Even though I knew I'd done the right thing, I still felt guilty and as if I'd betrayed her as I knew that was how she was going to see it.

'Well, I'm afraid she did, and inside your bag she found a considerable sum of money and three bags of white powder that she suspected were drugs,' Emma went on. 'She took it to the police station, and now they want us to take you there for questioning.'

'No,' Hannah gasped, shaking her head. 'No, you must be joking.'

She looked like she was about to cry.

'Why did you do this to me, Maggie?' she whimpered.

'I had to,' I told her. 'This is really serious, Hannah, and I had to report it. It's my job.'

She burst into tears and I put my hand on her shoulder.

'Hannah, you've got to start telling the truth. If you tell us what's been going on, we can try and help you,' I said gently. 'If someone put you up to this, we need to know who they are.'

'No,' she sobbed. 'I can't tell you.'

'I know you must be scared, Hannah, but we need to go to the police station now,' Emma told her gently.

Hannah looked shell-shocked as Emma stood up and pulled back the curtains from around her bed.

'You can come in my car and Maggie will meet us there,' she added. 'I'll be there with you when the police are questioning you.'

Hannah didn't say a word as she followed us down the ward. As we came out into the corridor, she suddenly stopped, her breathing ragged.

'Are you OK, lovey?' I asked.

'I'm sorry,' she mumbled and before we could stop her, she broke into a run.

Emma and I looked at each other in a panic as she bolted down the corridor. I couldn't just stand there and do nothing.

'Hannah, come back!' I yelled as I ran down the corridor after her. 'This is only going to make things worse!'

I turned round and saw Emma staggering behind me in her heels.

Thank God I put trainers on this morning, I thought to myself as I ran as fast as I could.

As I got a little further, I realised the end of the corridor was a dead end. Hannah was standing there with a look of complete panic on her face as her eyes darted round, desperately looking for an escape.

But there wasn't one. The game was up.

'Hannah,' I panted, completely out of breath. 'You can't run away anymore. You have to come and talk to the police, because if you don't, they will arrest you.'

'I can't, Maggie,' she whispered.

And with that, she slid down the wall, sank onto the floor and collapsed into a sobbing heap.

TEN

Nowhere to Hide

PC Williams paced up and down and I could see that she was rapidly losing patience.

I was back at the police station in the windowless, stark interview room and Hannah was being interviewed under caution.

She had been in floods of tears at the hospital and it had taken us ages to convince her to get into Emma's car.

'I know it's scary, lovey, but you really need to speak to the police,' I'd told her. 'You won't be on your own – Emma will be with you.'

Hannah's face had fallen.

'But I want you to be with me too,' she'd begged. 'Please Emma, can Maggie stay with me?'

I'd looked at Emma. Normally it would be a child's social worker who would sit in with them during a police interview as their appropriate adult.

'I'll have to check with the PC, but I don't see why two of us can't be there with you,' she'd said.

That had seemed to calm Hannah down a little bit; however, as we'd pulled up at the station, I could see that she was terrified.

'It's going to be OK,' I'd told her. 'Just tell the truth and we'll deal with whatever happens.'

But that wasn't happening. Hannah wasn't giving a straight answer to any of the questions and I could understand PC William's frustration.

She sat back down at the table.

'Hannah, I'm going to ask you again,' she said gently. 'Where did the money and the bags of drugs that Maggie found in your school bag come from?'

'I don't know,' she whispered.

'Did someone give them to you?' she asked. 'Were you going to sell them?'

'I don't know,' repeated Hannah. 'I don't know anything. Please stop asking me about it. I just want to go home.'

Her voice cracked, and all I wanted to do was pull her into a hug. But I knew she needed to talk.

'I really wish that I could, Hannah, but this is serious,' PC Williams told her firmly. 'We need to know where this money and these drugs have come from. Did someone put them in your bag and you didn't know that they were in there?'

Hannah buried her head in her hands.

'Please stop,' she whimpered. 'I can't do this . . . Maggie, tell her,' she begged, turning to me with her eyes filled with tears. 'Tell her how I've just come out of hospital.'

'Could she have a break and perhaps a glass of water?' I asked.

'Of course,' nodded PC Williams.

When she left the room, Hannah buried her head in her hands and sobbed. I put my arm around her and stroked her blonde hair. Whatever she'd done, she was still a vulnerable child.

'Why are you all doing this to me?' she wept, her shoulders shaking.

'Because you're being accused of some very serious things, Hannah, and the police need to get to the bottom of it,' Emma told her. 'I know you've been in hospital but you're lucky they didn't go up there and arrest you. You need to tell them what you know as you could be in danger too,' she urged. 'If you're not totally honest, this could end in you being charged and having to go to court. No one wants that.'

I knew it was harsh but Hannah needed to know the truth. She looked terrified and utterly distraught. Her life was spiralling out of control right in front of us.

'Emma's right, you have to tell them the truth,' I told her firmly. 'If you don't want to tell PC Williams what's going on, then please talk to us. If you do that, at least we can try and help you.'

'I can't,' she said firmly, shaking her head.

I couldn't understand who she was trying to protect or what kind of a hold they had on her that she was willing to risk everything by staying quiet.

After a short break PC Williams resumed the interview but it was clear that us talking to Hannah hadn't changed a thing and she wasn't going to answer any of her questions. We were getting nowhere fast.

'Please could I have a word with you both outside?' PC Williams asked.

'Of course,' said Emma.

Hannah looked terrified as the three of us stood up to leave the room.

'We'll be back in a minute, it's nothing to worry about,' I told her.

We stood in the corridor.

'It's clear we're not going to get anywhere today,' sighed PC Williams. 'Hannah's not willing to talk and I'm mindful of the fact that she has just come out of hospital and she's vulnerable. So for now, I'm not going to charge her but I do want her to come back to the station for further questioning in a couple of days.'

'Should she go back to school?' I asked her.

'I don't think it's a good idea for her to go anywhere on her own if possible,' she replied. 'I doubt that she's doing any of this alone and I don't want to give her the opportunity to warn off anyone else or to disappear given her track record. Maybe if we give her a little bit more time, she'll realise that it's in her best interests to talk to us.'

'I hope so,' I sighed.

I was worried about Hannah's safety. Whoever she was mixing with wasn't going to be happy that the drugs and money were gone and had been handed to the police.

Hannah just didn't strike me as a hardened drug dealer. She was either a very good liar or something was amiss here.

We all went back into the interview room.

'OK Hannah, we're going to leave it for today until you feel a little bit better,' PC Williams told her. 'But in a day or so, Maggie and Emma are going to bring you back here and I want you to be ready to tell me the truth.'

Hannah didn't say a word but I could see her shoulders sag with relief that she was leaving.

We all walked out of the police station and back to the car park. Hannah looked exhausted as she got into my car.

'I'm going to go and call Shelley now and let her know what's going on,' Emma told me. 'Let's keep in touch and I'll give you a ring later.'

Hannah and I drove home in silence. I think we were both shattered and relieved to be out of the police station. I knew Hannah had been through enough today and I didn't want to bombard her with more questions.

When we got back, she lay on the sofa and I fetched a blanket.

'Can I get you anything, flower?' I asked her but she shook her head and closed her eyes.

Shortly afterwards Emma called.

'How is she?' she asked.

'Absolutely exhausted,' I told her. 'But she seems glad to be back.'

'Has she said anything?' asked Emma.

'No and I'm not pushing her to. She's had enough questions for one day. I'm hoping that she'll start opening up to me in her own time.'

Emma had called Shelley and filled her in on what I'd found in Hannah's school bag.

'She was shocked and horrified,' she told me. 'She knew she was rebelling and going out and drinking but she never in a million years suspected that she was dealing drugs. In fact, she's struggling to believe it. She says Hannah has always been really anti-drugs, and this just isn't the Hannah that she knows.'

I think we all feel that way,' I replied.

When I'd finished talking to Emma, I checked on Hannah. She was fast asleep, curled up on the sofa. She looked so young and vulnerable as I tucked the blanket over her. She'd been through so much in the past forty-eight hours and I just wished that she would start opening up to us about what was happening so that we could try to help her. I was still struggling to believe that she was dealing drugs. The whole thing just didn't ring true to me.

While Hannah was having a nap, I decided to get on with some jobs around the house. Cleaning was my therapy and if I had something on my mind, it always helped to distract me and keep me busy. I cleaned the kitchen and the bathroom and while I was on a roll, I decided to change the sheets on my bed and Hannah's.

I stripped Hannah's bed first and then remade it with clean bedding. I stretched the fitted sheet across the corners of her bed but it kept pinging off.

'Arrghh, I hate this job,' I huffed to myself.

Finally I managed to do it, but as I was smoothing down the sheet, I heard something buzzing. Puzzled, I crouched down on the floor by the side of the bed and just as I did, I heard something buzz again. I looked under the bed but I couldn't see anything, so I tried lifting up the mattress and feeling underneath it but there was nothing there either. I was about to give up when something made me lift up the fitted sheet and feel down the side of the mattress. That's when I found it.

A slit had been cut in the side of the mattress to create a secret compartment. My heart was thumping as I tentatively pushed my hand in amongst the stuffing and the springs, unsure of what I was going to find in there. My hand felt something small and hard and I was surprised when I pulled it out to find that it was a phone. It wasn't Hannah's phone – she had a smartphone and this was a cheap pay-as-you-go kind, the ones that you can buy in those electronic stores on the high street. It vibrated again as a text flashed up on the screen.

Keep yr mouth shut bitch u know wat will happen if u talk.

As I read the message, I felt sick to my stomach. I needed to see more of exactly what was on this phone and why Hannah had hidden it, but I didn't have the code to unlock it. I typed in the most obvious one, not thinking for one moment that it would actually work.

1234.

I couldn't believe it when the screen miraculously sprung into life. I went straight to contacts and there was only one number and name stored there – Lenny.

It was a name that I didn't recognise and Hannah had never mentioned him.

Who on earth was Lenny?

There were several calls mainly made late at night but there were endless texts.

My hands were shaking as I quickly scrolled through them. They went back over the previous four months – far longer than the time Hannah had been at my house. They were mainly a series of instructions, meeting places and times.

B @ station. 3.30 p.m train. Bring bag.

Hannah had sometimes replied.

Can't b that long. M thinks I'm at athletics.

U think I care bitch. B there.

I shuddered as I read through them. The language and the way this person spoke to Hannah was horrendous.

Party 2nite. Same place.

Can't go, Hannah had written.

B there or u no what will happen.

I will hve 2 sneak out when M is asleep, Hannah had replied.

It was like a vital piece of the puzzle had been slotted into place.

One look at this phone told me everything I needed to know. This Lenny person was the one Hannah had been hanging around with for the past four months. The pair had arranged to meet in the middle of the day when Hannah was supposed to be at school, or after school when she'd told me that she was at athletics. All those nights when Hannah had come back drunk or high suddenly made sense. He was the puppet master and she was his puppet. But how and why?

I knew I had to confront Hannah about this. It was time for her to tell me the truth.

As I went downstairs, I felt the churn of nerves in my stomach. How was she going to react when she found out that I'd discovered her secret?

As I walked in the living room, Hannah had just started to stir on the sofa. She stretched out and yawned sleepily. I sat down beside her as she rubbed her eyes.

'Hannah . . .' I said gently, trying to keep my voice calm and steady. 'Who is Lenny?'

Hannah sprung up from the sofa like she'd just had an electric shock.

'Who is he, Hannah?' I asked again. 'Please tell me.'

'How do you know about Lenny?' she asked, looking stricken. 'Has he been round here looking for me?'

It was clear she was terrified out of her wits.

I reached into my pocket and put the pay-as-you-go phone on the coffee table. All of the colour drained from her face and she looked like she was about to be sick.

'W-w-where did you get that?' she stammered. 'That's mine. It's private.'

'I was changing your sheets when I heard it buzz,' I explained. 'I felt the mattress and I found your hiding place.'

I put my hand on her arm.

'Hannah, I've read your messages and seen the horrendous way this Lenny talks to you,' I told her. 'Who is he? You've got to tell me.'

'I can't,' she whispered, shaking her head, her hair covering her face as she refused to meet my eyes.

'You have to,' I urged. 'Hannah, whatever you're mixed up in is really serious and I'm worried that you're in real danger. You're already in serious trouble with the police. You need to talk to me, otherwise things are only going to get worse.

'Do you want me to call Emma?' I asked. 'Will you talk to her?'

'No,' she snapped. 'I don't want her to know anything.'

'Hannah, so many people love you and are worried about you – your mum, Molly, me and Emma. You have to start talking to us, lovey. You have to tell us the truth. This has gone too far now, and you're in too deep. From Lenny's texts, it sounds as though your life could be in danger.

'If you tell me the truth then I can try to help you,' I told her, squeezing her hand. 'You don't have to carry this stress and worry all by yourself anymore. I can't imagine how hard that must be.'

She shook her head tearfully.

'I can help you but you have to trust me, OK?'

She nodded.

'So please, please just tell me who this Lenny person is, Hannah,' I begged.

Hannah looked at the floor.

'I can't,' she sobbed, shaking her head. 'I can't tell you anything.'

'But why not?' I pleaded.

She burst into tears.

'Because if I do, he'll hurt Molly, OK? He'll hurt Molly and Mum, just like he's hurt me.'

ELEVEN

Time for the Truth

I pulled Hannah to me and put my arm around her. Her whole body was shaking as she sobbed.

'Hannah, you have to tell me what's going on,' I urged her. 'I really want to help but you need to tell me.'

Her eyes filled with tears again.

'Lenny's my boyfriend,' she sniffed.

My heart sank. They were the words that I'd been expecting but also dreading. No boyfriend should talk to someone the way this man had spoken to Hannah in his texts.

But as she spoke, I bit my lip and didn't show any reaction. I needed her to talk and I was so scared that if I said or did the wrong thing, she would clam up and shut down again.

'Where did you meet him?' I asked gently.

She wiped her eyes with a trembling hand and gave me a weak smile.

'It sounds lame, but him and his mate Lee started talking to me on the bus back from school,' she replied.

'He was good-looking and funny but I didn't think any more of it.

'Then he was on the same bus a few days later and then again the week after that,' she continued.

'It's really corny but he said it was meant to be that we kept bumping into each other like that.'

'Did you like him?' I asked.

Hannah nodded.

'He was cool and nice to me and told me I was pretty,' she said shyly. 'Then one time when I saw him again, he said instead of chatting on buses why didn't we go for a milkshake at McDonald's. So I said OK. I suppose I couldn't believe he was interested in me. He seemed so grown up – not like the boys at school.'

Hannah described how she'd texted him her number and they had met up one Saturday afternoon in town.

'I didn't tell Mum or Molly,' she shrugged. 'I don't know why. I think cos he was older than me and Mum was at work so it was easier not to tell her than for her to ask loads of questions.'

'How old is Lenny?' I asked.

She shrugged her shoulders.

'I didn't ask, but I thought maybe nineteen or something. He definitely looked older and he said he had a car.

'He was really nice,' she smiled. 'He was funny and chatty and he seemed to really care about me. He told me how pretty and clever I was, and he really listened. And he bought me presents, too.'

'What sort of presents?' I asked, intrigued.

'Really nice stuff,' she said. 'He gave me some Chanel perfume that first time in McDonald's, some expensive make-up and then another time a pair of Nikes.'

I remembered the expensive trainers that Charlie had noticed when Hannah had first come to live with me.

'I'm not surprised you were impressed,' I told her. 'It sounds like he swept you off your feet.'

'He did . . .' she nodded, then paused. '. . . at first.'

Hannah's voice trailed off and she looked down at the floor. She started picking nervously at her nails.

'What happened after that?' I asked her gently.

She shook her head.

'I don't want to talk about it,' she mumbled.

I reached for her hand but she wouldn't look at me.

'Hannah, I know this is really hard but if you want me to help you then you need to talk to me,' I told her. 'You're doing really well . . .

'Please Hannah,' I begged. 'Tell me what happened then.'

I was relieved when she cleared her throat and started to talk.

'I met Lenny at McDonald's a few times, then one time he invited me to a party,' she told me. 'I was excited cos I'd never been to a proper party before.'

'Did you tell your mum?' I asked.

She quickly shook her head.

'No, there's no way Mum would have let me go if I'd told her, so I said I was going round to Lizzie's that night. She knows Lizzie so she didn't mind.

'Lenny picked me up at the end of the road so she wouldn't see his car.'

Hannah described how the party was at Lenny's mate Lee's flat.

'I didn't like it,' she said. 'I didn't know anyone, everyone was drinking and Lenny left me on my own. I was upset so I went and found Lenny and told him I was going,' she continued. 'But I didn't know where I was so he said he would drive me.

'But we didn't go home.'

'Where did you go?' I asked.

She described how Lenny had driven her out to the countryside in the middle of nowhere. He'd apologised for ignoring her at the party.

'Then he told me that he loved me and that he had a present for me and he gave me a phone,' she told me. 'I said I couldn't take it but he said it meant we could keep in touch without my mum knowing.'

'Is that the phone that I found?' I asked.

Hannah nodded sheepishly.

'I really liked him, Maggie,' she sighed. 'He was always telling me how pretty I was. He was so much nicer to me than any of the boys at school ever were.'

Then Lenny had driven her home.

'After that he messaged me loads on my new phone,' she said. 'He was always texting me saying nice things and asking when he could take me out.'

Over the next few weeks Hannah had continued to see Lenny.

He'd told her not to tell her mum as she might stop them seeing each other because he was older.

'So I kept it a secret,' she said. 'I didn't tell anyone, not even Molly. I'd tell Mum I was at a friend's house or sometimes I'd climb out of the window at night after she and Molly had gone to bed and Lenny would pick me up.'

'Where would you go?' I asked.

'We'd drive out to the countryside and we'd look at the stars and chat and stuff,' she sighed.

I took a deep breath and asked the question that I was dreading the answer to.

'Hannah, did he have sex with you?'

She blushed and looked down at the ground.

Then she nodded.

'I didn't want to at first, but he told me how much he loved me, how beautiful I was, and that he wanted to show me how special I was. After that first time I was scared that he wouldn't want anything to do with me anymore and I'd never see him again.

'But then he texted the next day saying how amazing I was and how he couldn't live without me. He said he loved me, and I knew then that I loved him too.'

I shuddered inside. I could see how this young, naïve girl had been completely taken in by this older, good-looking man. I could see how this was spiralling and I almost didn't want to hear the rest, even though I knew I had to.

'Maggie?' Hannah asked, as though suddenly coming back to the present. 'Can I have a drink?'

'Of course you can, lovey,' I told her.

I suddenly felt really guilty. I could see how exhausted Hannah was after all that talking and I was mindful of the fact that she had just come out of hospital and had been interviewed by the police already today. I was relieved that she had opened up to me at all about Lenny but I wanted her to keep going.

We went into the kitchen and she sat down at the table. I poured us both an apple juice.

'Do you want something to eat?' I asked her. 'You didn't have any lunch.'

'I'm not hungry,' she sighed.

I sat down at the table next to her and we sipped our drinks in silence. I desperately wanted to ask Hannah more questions but I didn't want her to feel like I was interrogating her. However, without any prompting from me, she began to talk again.

'A few months ago, there was another party at Lee's,' she said in a small voice. 'I didn't want to go after the last one, but Lenny persuaded me. Everyone was doing shots again and Lenny gave me one and they were all looking at me so I downed it too. I didn't want him to think I was young and babyish and finish with me.

'I don't know how many I had but I remember trying to find the toilet to be sick and people were laughing at me. I felt dizzy and my head was all fuzzy and I just wanted to go home.'

Her voice wobbled with emotion and I could see she was shaking.

She took a deep breath.

'I couldn't find Lenny anywhere and I felt so sick so I lay down on the couch. The next thing I knew I felt hands all over me, touching me and pulling at my clothes. When I opened my eyes, I could see it wasn't Lenny. It was Lee and he was pulling my dress up and putting his fingers inside me.

'I was shouting and screaming for Lenny to come and help and get Lee off me and I was so relieved when I saw him cos I thought he would punch him or something.

'But he was laughing, Maggie. He could see what Lee was doing to me and he just stood there watching and laughing and filming it on his phone.'

Tears streamed down her cheeks.

'I tried so hard to fight him off but I couldn't,' she sobbed. 'I wanted to scream and shout and scratch and kick him but I couldn't move. It was like I was in my body but I wasn't. I knew these things were happening to me but I couldn't do anything to stop it.

'And then after Lee, Lenny was on top of me too. It was like it wasn't real but I know it was cos then I woke up on the couch and I had no knickers on and my dress was all ripped and I was really, really sore down there, you know down below,' she said, embarrassed.

I could see the pain and the distress on her face and my heart broke for her. It was utterly horrifying hearing the horrendous things that she had gone through.

'Oh Hannah,' I soothed. 'I'm so, so sorry. I had no idea.'

'Why would you?' she sobbed. 'I didn't tell anybody.

'Lenny just put me in his car and drove me home like nothing had happened. I couldn't stop crying but he told me I was being pathetic. He dragged me out and left me on the doorstep in the middle of the night. I didn't have a key so I had to bang on the door and Mum let me in.

'She was so angry that I had sneaked out and the next day I couldn't go to school, I couldn't get out of bed. I felt awful and I just kept crying.

'I wondered if I had dreamt it but I knew I hadn't. And I wanted to tell her but I knew she would have been even more angry with me.'

Hannah described how she'd made the decision never to see Lenny again. He'd continually texted and rung her but she hadn't replied, then he'd turned up on the bus home from school.

'He was crying and telling me he loved me. He told me how sorry he was and he kept begging me for a second chance,' she told me. 'He'd bought me some posh chocolates and a new rucksack.'

She shrugged.

'I didn't know what to do. I'd never had a boyfriend before so I said I'd see him again.

'Things were fine for a bit, and he was really kind to me. We spent a lot of time just hanging out together, and he bought me more presents, but then there were more parties and it was easier to just give in and join in with it rather than fighting against it.

'They put stuff in my drink. I knew that's what they must have done the first time too, that's why my head felt so fuzzy and strange and why I couldn't do anything to stop them.

'In a way, it was better that way. Lenny and his mates could do what they wanted to me and I could just black out.'

Whereas she had been in tears before, she was now almost emotionless as she recounted the terrible things that had been done to her. I was the one close to tears as I listened to her tell her story. She was still a child, for God's sake, and yet she had been treated so horrendously, passed around by grown men like a plaything to be used and abused.

'Hannah, why didn't you tell someone about what Lenny was doing? They could have helped you to put a stop to it,' I asked gently.

'It's hard to explain,' she sighed. 'I didn't think I had a choice, and I couldn't get away from him. He was texting me all the time, day and night. He was outside school in his car waiting for me. He was outside my bedroom window at night and I'd see him driving past the house constantly.

'I was really scared of him by now and it felt like there was no way out of it.

'I didn't think it could get any worse but then it did.'

Hannah described how one afternoon after he had picked her up from school, he'd handed her a package.

'It was thick brown envelope,' she said. 'He told me I had to bunk off school the next day and get on a train to a seaside town about an hour away and drop the package off for him. I asked him what was in it but he said it was none of my business and gave me all these instructions about where I was supposed to leave it. He said I'd be less likely to be stopped because I was a girl.

'I'm not stupid, Maggie. I knew whatever was in that parcel wasn't going to be good or legal so I told him I wasn't going to do it. And that's when he told me . . .' her voice cracked with emotion again.

She took a deep breath.

'That's when he said he had videos on his phone of me having sex with him and his friends. And if I didn't do what he said, he would send them to everyone that I knew, including everyone at school, and Mum and Molly.

'I didn't have a choice, Maggie. I vowed it would be just the once so I did it.'

Hannah described how she had gone into school as normal the next day. She'd been marked in by the register then mid-morning she'd snuck out with some sixth-formers and headed to the station. Lenny had already bought her a return ticket.

'I'd worked out that if I missed a couple of lessons and then lunch it meant I had three hours to get there and back and be back in time for the last lesson,' she said.

'Who did you give the package to?' I asked her.

'I didn't give it to anyone,' she explained.

Lenny had told her the plan was to leave the package in a litterbin in a little park outside the station.

'I dropped it in the bin as I walked past and then went back into the station. Lenny said someone would be waiting to pick it up but I never saw anyone. Then I got back on the train and went back to school like nothing had ever happened.'

That night Hannah had snuck out to his flat to tell Lenny she had done what he'd asked.

'Then he said he'd have another package for me to drop off the week after,' she said. 'But I told him no. I said I didn't want to do it anymore, and that I didn't want to see him again.

'He got really angry and told me I had to do it and if I didn't or if I told anyone, then he and his friends would hurt Molly.'

Hannah started to cry.

'He told me him and his mates knew which school she went to, the way she walked home, the names of her friends.

'They could hurt me but I couldn't let them hurt Mol,' she sobbed.

Hannah described how, over the next few months, she'd delivered several more packages for Lenny. She'd bunk off school or go straight afterwards or late at night. She still had to go to the parties where she would have to report back to Lenny.

'When I got put into care and came to your house, I thought maybe I had a way out, perhaps it would stop. But I still had Lenny's phone and he was constantly texting and ringing me. I ignored it, thinking he'd get bored eventually.

'Then Molly came to contact with a broken arm and I just knew it was never going to be over.'

'Lenny did that?' I gasped, horrified.

Hannah nodded tearfully.

'Yeah, Lenny or someone that he knows,' she sobbed. 'He'd been to my house and knew I wasn't there any more so hurting Molly was a warning sign for me not to tell.

'When Molly came to that first contact with a broken arm, I knew then I could never have contact with her and Mum again in case Lenny followed them here. If he did that, then he would know where I was.

'I don't know how, but he found out where my new school is and that was bad enough. One afternoon he was waiting outside for me and it just started all over again. I had to skip school in the day to deliver his packages or after school when I'd told you I was at athletics.'

I couldn't even begin to imagine the fear this poor girl must have felt over the past few months. She'd been groomed, raped and forced into drug dealing. She was just a child. It was one of the most horrifying things that I'd ever heard.

But as Hannah continued to talk, one terrifying thought suddenly came into my head.

'Hannah, does Lenny know the address here?' I asked her. 'Has he ever picked you up from this house or dropped you off here?'

Because if he had, we were both in grave danger.

TWELVE

Questions

My heart thumped out of my chest as I waited for Hannah's reply.

When she shook her head, I breathed out a huge sigh of relief.

'I didn't want Lenny to know where I was so I made sure I never gave him this address,' she said firmly. 'When I went into care, I told him Social Services had put me in a children's home to throw him off the scent, but it didn't take him long to find out what school I was at, and I didn't want him turning up here every night like he used to do at my house.'

Clever girl, I thought to myself.

If Lenny had known my address, I knew there would be enough concern for her safety that Social Services would have to move Hannah to another carer immediately. She'd already had so much upheaval and after everything she'd just disclosed to me and the horrific ordeal that she'd been through, I wanted to try to support her through this.

'I always made sure I met him somewhere or he picked me up outside school,' she added. 'Even when I went to one of the parties, somehow I got myself home and I've always checked no one was following me.'

I thought back to the way Hannah would look out of the front window when she came in from school and close the living-room curtains when it was still light. For months the poor girl had been living in fear of Lenny finding her or following her here.

'He knows Mum's address though, and where Molly's school is, so he can still get to them any time he wants,' she sighed.

I could see that she was genuinely terrified of this man.

'Hannah, I'm so sorry you've had to cope with all of this on your own,' I told her, taking her hand. 'I can't even begin to imagine what that must have felt like.'

There was still so much I wanted to ask her about, in particular the events of the past couple of days.

'What happened to you the other night when you ended up in hospital?' I asked.

Hannah explained how Lenny had given her a package to deliver that day.

'I knew I had three hours from when school finished to when you were picking me up after you'd thought I'd been to athletics,' she told me. 'But when I got off the train, the little park where the bin was, where I was supposed to put the package, was all taped off.

'There were builders digging it up. I panicked – I didn't know what to do. Lenny had told me never to use the phone to talk or text about the deliveries so I couldn't call him.

'All I could do was come back. Then the trains were all delayed so I knew I wouldn't be back in time for you to pick me up and I panicked even more.'

When Hannah's train had eventually got in, she had gone round to Lenny's flat to tell him what had happened.

'His mates were there and he'd been drinking,' she told me. 'He was angry. He was yelling, saying the people who were expecting the package weren't happy.

'I told him there had been a mix-up and there was nothing I could do, but I don't think he believed me, Maggie. He said I'd have to bunk off school and take it the next day instead.'

As she spoke, my mind was ticking over, thinking about the police and possible evidence. I had to be upfront with her.

'Hannah, I'm so sorry to have to ask you this,' I said gently. 'But did Lenny or any of his friends have sex with you the other night?'

She shook her head.

'He got his kicks that night from hurting me instead,' she sighed, shuddering at the memory. 'Lenny said he was going to teach me a lesson for messing him about.

'He shouted and screamed at me in front of everyone, telling me how useless I was, and then he burnt me with cigarettes and made me down vodka until I thought I was going to pass out. There must have been something in it because I couldn't stand up or move. They were all just laughing at me. Then one of his mates drove me out into the countryside, punched me in the face and threw me out of the car.'

'Oh Hannah,' I sighed. 'I'm so sorry.'

'Whatever drug they'd spiked my drink with was so strong, I couldn't do anything,' she mumbled. 'I knew what was happening but I couldn't move or make a noise. I was so scared. I just shut my eyes and thought I was going to die there on my own in the cold and dark.'

Hannah was almost emotionless now. It was like she was so exhausted that she had no tears left.

I put my arms around her.

'It's over now,' I soothed, giving her a hug. 'You've been so, so brave. But what I need to do now is call Emma and tell her everything that you've just told me,' I added.

Hannah's face crumpled and I could see the fear in her eyes.

'You can't do that, Maggie,' she pleaded, looking terrified. 'Lenny will find out that I've told and then he'll hurt Molly and Mum.

'Please Maggie,' she begged. 'You can't tell anyone.'

'Lovey, I have to,' I told her, trying to calm her down. 'I haven't got a choice. It's my job to keep you safe and now you've told me this information I have to pass it on to your social worker, and Emma will need to talk to the police.'

Hannah looked absolutely broken.

'No!' she yelled. 'That's not fair. You said I could trust you.'

She was sobbing now, her head in her hands.

'And you can, Hannah,' I replied. 'But everyone needs to know what's going on. You're at risk of being charged with a serious offence and it's important that the police know that you were forced into it. And they will need to speak to Lenny about everything that he's done to you.'

'But what about Mum and Molly?' cried Hannah.

'If you tell the police the full story then they can help to protect them,' I told her.

'I'll talk to Emma and I'll put it on loud speaker so you can hear exactly what I'm telling her then you can step in if I'm getting anything wrong, OK?'

Hannah nodded. She looked utterly drained.

When I got through to Emma, I explained about finding the mobile phone hidden in Hannah's bedroom.

'When I asked her about it, she disclosed some information to me that I need to pass on to you straight away,' I told her.

In a very calm and straightforward way, I went through the whole horrendous sequence of events. I told her about Lenny and how Hannah had met him and how he had groomed and raped her, and recently how she had been forced to deliver packages for him. As I repeated it all, I almost had to disassociate myself from it. I stuck to the facts as that was what Emma needed and it wouldn't have done Hannah any good for me to become upset.

As foster carers, we're taught to give facts rather than become emotional or pass judgement when we're sharing or recording information. But it was still horrific having to say these things out loud to Emma while Hannah was listening. As I was talking, she still had her head in her hands, and silent tears were running down her cheeks. I reached over and held her hand and gave it a quick squeeze to reassure her.

I could tell Emma was doing her best to remain calm and emotionless too but I could still hear the shock in her voice as I repeated what Hannah had told me.

'Well done, Hannah,' she said when I'd finished detailing everything Hannah had told me. 'You've been unbelievably brave. I'm going to give PC Williams a ring now and speak to her about where we go from here.'

'Do you really have to tell the police?' asked Hannah, looking terrified.

'We have to,' Emma told her. 'There is no other option.'

Before I hung up, I took the phone into the living room to have a quiet word with Emma out of Hannah's earshot.

'Oh Maggie,' she sighed, once I'd switched her off speaker-phone. 'That poor girl. It's horrific. I never imagined for one second that's what was happening.'

'I know,' I replied. 'I felt like crying when she told me. It's unbearable thinking that she's been carrying that around with her, too scared to talk to anyone or get help.'

Sadly, I'd fostered many children in the past who had been raped and sexually abused but I'd never had to deal with a situation like this before where a child had been groomed and exploited.

My fostering training had taught me that when a child was disclosing something of this magnitude to you, you should try to remain impartial and calm and let them talk. I still had so many questions but for now they would have to wait. Hannah had been through enough.

Once I got off the phone to Emma, I rang my supervising social worker, Becky, to let her know what Hannah had told me. She was equally as shocked and horrified.

'Keep in touch and let me know how this unfolds,' she told me. 'And if you need someone to talk it through with, you know where I am.'

'Thank you, Becky,' I replied. 'I'm still trying to get my head around it all to be honest, and to be as supportive as I can for Hannah.'

Half an hour later Emma called back.

'I spoke to PC Williams and she'd like you to bring Hannah back down to the station today to make another statement,' she told me.

'But she's exhausted,' I said.

'I know, but she was adamant they need to speak to Hannah today,' she replied. 'She's made some serious allegations to you, Maggie, and PC Williams wants to record them just in case she clams up again or changes her mind.'

'Are they not going to take her to a safe house to be questioned?' I asked.

When a child had been sexually abused or raped, they tended to be interviewed at a safe house rather than a police station. Our local one looked like an ordinary house and there were interview rooms there with sofas and a kitchen. There was also a medical room where they could be examined by a doctor.

'At this stage I don't think so,' she said. 'Unfortunately it sounds like there's not going to be any DNA or physical evidence that they can take from Hannah at this point. At the moment it's very much her statement that's needed and the police can take it from her there.

'I'll also need to contact Shelley and let her know what's happened,' she added.

My heart sank. If I'd found it hard to listen to what Hannah had been through, I knew this was going to tear Shelley apart.

'I'm sure she'll want to see Hannah but we need to check that's OK with her,' said Emma. 'As we know, Hannah hasn't wanted contact with her mum for the past few months.'

'Well we know now that's because she was trying to protect her,' I told her. 'She didn't want to risk seeing her and Molly after she realised Lenny had broken Molly's arm.'

'Maybe she could come round this evening or even tomorrow to see Hannah?' she suggested.

'I don't think it's a good idea for Shelley or Molly to come here,' I told her. 'After everything Hannah has told us about this Lenny and what happened with the failed drop the other day, there's a real risk that he could be following them.'

'That's true,' sighed Emma. 'We're going to have to tread very carefully.'

When I put down the phone, I knew I would have to tell Hannah. Her face fell when I said we had to go back to the police station so she could be re-interviewed.

'All you have to do is tell them what you have just told me,' I urged. 'You've been so brave, Hannah, you can do this. Emma and I will be with you every step of the way.'

Before we left, I made her a cheese sandwich.

'You've got to try and eat something,' I told her gently.

'I'm not hungry,' she said, pushing it away. 'I feel sick.'

The most I could get her to have was a glass of milk and a biscuit.

I put the mobile Lenny had given Hannah into my bag as I knew I'd have to hand it in to the police like I'd done with the drugs and money in case they needed it for evidence. But as we walked out of the door, I felt it vibrate and heard the distinct ping that signified a text had arrived. Hannah's face drained of colour.

'That's him, isn't it?' she gasped. 'He'll be going crazy, Maggie. I've disappeared with his drugs and his money and I haven't delivered them like I was supposed to yesterday.'

I quickly glanced at the text and shuddered.

Where the f**k r u? I am gonna f***ing kill you b*tch, and that little sister of yours.

'What's he saying?' she asked, her eyes wide with fear.

I couldn't tell her. I was worried that fear would stop her from telling the truth to the police.

But she knew Lenny and I couldn't lie to her either.

'You're right,' I sighed. 'He's angry that you've gone AWOL and he wants to know where you are.

'The only thing you can do now is tell the police everything,' I told her calmly. 'They will help make sure that you're safe and we'll hand the phone in to them too so they can deal with it.'

'But what about Mum and Molly?' she cried. 'I know what Lenny's like. He doesn't care if he hurts them.'

'Let's talk to the police,' I repeated, keeping my voice steady.

I was trying to remain calm on the outside for Hannah but on the inside I had a growing sense of unease. She was involved with some nasty people and where drugs and money were concerned, people were prepared to do anything.

By the time we pulled up in the car park near to the police station, I could see the terror on Hannah's face. I opened the passenger door but she hesitated.

'Come on, flower,' I soothed. 'Emma will be waiting.'

Finally she got out of the car but as we walked down the high street, I could see she was jumpy and on edge and constantly looking around, even though her jacket hood was pulled up, covering her face.

I linked my arm through hers, feeling her trembling as we walked along.

'You can do this,' I said, giving her a weak smile.

Emma and PC Williams were waiting for us in reception.

'You're doing the right thing, Hannah,' Emma told her, putting her hand on her shoulder. 'You're being incredibly brave.'

141

'Thanks for coming back in, Hannah,' PC Williams told her.

She led us through to the same grotty interview room where a woman in her thirties in a black trouser suit was sitting.

'This is my colleague DC Doherty from CID,' she told her. 'She's going to sit in on the interview today and we're also going to tape it.'

I'd already handed the mobile phone that Lenny had given Hannah in to reception and a PC had bagged it up and labelled it. Emma and I sat on chairs either side of Hannah.

As PC Williams started to question her, I expected Hannah to cry but she didn't. They were asking her the most intimate, traumatic questions but she was devoid of any emotion. It seemed that, at this point, switching herself off was the only way that she could cope.

I was so proud of her as she told them everything that she knew. She gave them dates, addresses, details about Lenny's flat and detailed every single horrific encounter she'd had with him and his friends.

'Were there any other girls at the flat when you went round there?' PC Williams asked.

'A couple,' replied Hannah. 'But I think they were much older.'

PC Williams had thankfully been very gentle with her but DC Doherty was a lot more aggressive.

'Did you know what was in the packages that Lenny asked you to deliver?'

Hannah shook her head.

'You must have had a look?' she asked. 'Surely you knew it must have been something illegal.'

'I didn't want to know,' whispered Hannah. 'It was better that way. I just did what Lenny asked me. I was too frightened not to. He'd told me what he was prepared to do. He was going to hurt my family so I had no choice.'

Tears spilled out of her eyes and she started to cry. It was the only time that she'd broken down during the whole interview.

I could see how much pain she was in and I desperately wanted to put my arm around her and comfort her but I knew I couldn't. Emma and I were just observers, sitting in on the interview, and I didn't want to do anything that risked distracting her from the police's questions.

After another hour of questioning, it was finally over. Hannah looked utterly drained, and I could only imagine how exhausted she must feel.

'Hannah, you're free to go now,' DC Doherty told her. 'We'll keep in touch with your social worker.'

'Maggie, if you take Hannah and wait outside, I'll just have a quick word with PC Williams,' Emma told me.

As we came out of the interview room, I could see Hannah's shoulders visibly sag with relief.

I gave her a hug.

'You must be absolutely shattered,' I told her. 'You did so well. Well done.'

A few minutes later Emma came out of the interview room and joined us.

'Let's get you out of here,' she said kindly.

As we walked down the corridor to the reception area, a figure was waiting there.

'Mum!' gasped Hannah.

Emma and I looked at each other.

'She wasn't supposed to be here,' hissed Emma.

I knew she had wanted to check that Hannah was happy to see Shelley first. But we needn't have worried. As soon as Hannah saw her mum, she ran towards her and collapsed into her arms, sobbing.

THIRTEEN

The Fallout

Hannah buried her face in her mum's shoulder and wept.

Tears streamed down Shelley's face too.

'Hannah, my love, I'm so, so sorry,' she cried, stroking the back of her head. 'I had no idea.'

'I'm sorry too,' Hannah sniffed. 'I should have told you but I was so scared.'

'Well, there's no need to be scared any more,' she told her. 'We'll work this out together, I promise. I won't let anyone hurt you ever again.'

Shelley turned to Emma.

'I'm sorry for turning up without any notice like this,' she told her. 'When you described what Hannah had said, every horrendous thing she'd been through, I just needed to see her and hug her. I knew you were coming down here and I couldn't wait.'

She looked at Hannah.

'I didn't even know if you'd want to see me,' she told her, her voice trembling.

'Of course I do,' Hannah replied, clinging to her mum. 'I only said I didn't cos I was worried Lenny or one of his mates would follow you to Maggie's house then they'd know where I was.

'When I knew they'd broken Molly's arm I was just so frightened. I thought it would be better for you and Molly if you didn't see me anymore, that way they'd leave you alone.'

Shelley looked puzzled.

'What, they did that to your sister?' she gasped.

Hannah nodded.

'It was a message to me. When I saw her arm in plaster when you came round to Maggie's house, I knew it wasn't safe for me to see you both anymore.'

'Oh Hannah,' sighed Shelley, tears filling her eyes again. 'My poor baby.'

We were still in the busy reception area of the police station and there were people coming in and out.

'Why don't we go somewhere else and you two can have a proper chat?' suggested Emma.

'I'm happy to come back to your house, Maggie, if that would work?' replied Shelley.

Hannah looked panicked and shook her head straight away.

'I think it's best if we go somewhere else,' said Emma swiftly. 'Why don't we all go back to my office?

'There are lots of contact rooms there. I'm sure one of them will be free and you two can have a cup of tea and spend a bit of time together.'

Shelley nodded and Hannah looked relieved. Social Services was based in a large modern building in the town centre that was a ten-minute drive from the police station.

Shelley came in the car with me. She insisted on sitting in the back with Hannah and as I drove along, I looked in the rear-view mirror to see Hannah's head resting on her mum's shoulder. If anything good had come out of this at all, it was that mother and daughter had been reunited.

When we got to Social Services, one of the contact rooms was free so we got Hannah and Shelley settled and made them a cup of tea.

'What about Molly?' asked Hannah. 'Do we have to tell her what's happened?'

'I think we need to be honest with her,' nodded Shelley. 'She's thirteen so she's old enough to understand.

'She took it very badly when you said that you didn't want to see us. She adores you, Hannah, and she was so hurt. I think that telling her what was really going on behind the scenes is important to help her understand.

'Don't worry, I'll talk to her.'

Emma and I left them to it and we went to her office for a chat.

'So what did the police say?' I asked her.

'They're going to arrest Lenny West and bring him in for questioning,' she told me. 'I'm assuming that they will search his flat too. PC Williams has promised to keep me updated.'

I knew nothing was going to happen quickly as it was a complicated investigation with two strands – the drugs and the grooming. Both were going to take time to look into.

'I'll keep you posted, Maggie,' Emma told me.

'In the meantime, what should we do about school?' I asked her.

'I don't think it's safe for her to go back there again,' sighed Emma. 'Lenny knows that's where she goes so he and his mates could turn up at any point. I'll put the wheels in motion to get a home tutor organised.'

We chatted a little more, and soon it was time to collect Hannah.

'We need to go, I'm afraid,' I told her. 'You must be absolutely shattered after everything you've been through today.'

As if on cue, she gave a huge yawn.

'Oh Han, go back and try to get some sleep,' Shelley told her, stroking her hair.

But I could see Hannah was reluctant to leave her.

'Can I see you again?' she asked, looking very young all of a sudden.

She and Shelley both looked at Emma expectantly.

'Of course you can,' Emma told her. 'We can restart contact straight away if you'd both like. We'll book one of these rooms for you so you can spend some time together.'

'And Molly too?' asked Hannah eagerly.

'Yes,' nodded Emma. 'If she wants to. I'll try and sort something out for tomorrow if you'd like?'

As she got up to go, Hannah started to cry.

'I don't want to leave you,' she sobbed to Shelley. 'I've missed you so much, Mum. I'm so sorry.'

'Hey, don't cry,' Shelley soothed, giving her a hug. 'I've missed you too and hopefully I'll see you tomorrow. You've been so brave today and I'm so proud of you.'

Hannah nodded through her tears.

'I love you, darling,' Shelley told her as we left the room.

In the lift I put my arm around Hannah.

She sagged against me, letting me hug her close.

'It must have been nice to see your mum again,' I smiled. 'You can tell she really cares about you to turn up like that.'

She nodded.

In the car home, Hannah was silent. I was exhausted so I couldn't even begin to imagine how she must be feeling after such a traumatic and emotionally draining day.

'What do you fancy for dinner?' I asked her when we got in.

'I'm not hungry,' she sighed. 'I just want to go to bed.'

'OK, sweetie,' I nodded.

It was only eight thirty and it was still light outside but I could see that Hannah was wiped out. Ten minutes later I went up to say goodnight and knocked on her bedroom door. Hannah was already in her pyjamas and lying in bed.

'Maggie, I'm really tired but I'm too scared to sleep,' she sighed. 'I keep thinking about Lenny and what he's going to do when he gets arrested by the police. They're going to ask him about me so he's going to know it's me that's told on him.'

I stroked her blonde hair back from her forehead.

'Hannah, you've done the right thing,' I told her. 'The police know what he's done and we're all going to do our very best to protect you.

'Remember, whatever happens, he doesn't know where you are so you're safe here.'

She nodded sleepily.

I said goodnight and went downstairs. I was shattered, not just physically but emotionally, and I hadn't got the head-space to concentrate on anything. All I could think about was Hannah and how she was and I left it fifteen minutes before I crept back upstairs to check on her.

As I peered around her door, I was relieved to see that she was already in a deep sleep. As I watched her lying there, there was a lump in my throat. She looked so young and fragile. Even at fifteen, she was still a child and it made me so angry to think about what she had been subjected to over these past few months. She had been used and abused in the most appalling way and sadly this trauma was something that would stay with her and affect her for the rest of her life.

'Don't you worry, flower,' I whispered in the darkness. 'We'll get the monster that did this to you.'

I went downstairs and as soon as I flopped onto the sofa, my phone rang. It was Louisa and although I felt bad, I didn't answer it. To be honest, I didn't want to speak to anybody. I'd been talking and processing all day and I didn't have the energy or the headspace for anything else.

By ten o'clock I gave up and went up to bed. So many thoughts were whizzing around my brain, I was worried I wasn't going to be able to sleep. But as soon as my head hit the pillow, I was out like a light.

It was the piercing scream that woke me. Even though I was still half asleep, my instincts kicked in immediately. Within seconds I grabbed my phone, leapt out of bed and, my heart pounding in fear, I raced down the landing in the dark to Hannah's room.

Had Lenny somehow found us?

'Get off me!' I heard her yell. 'You're hurting me. I'll kill you.'

I could hardly breathe as I flicked on the landing light and pushed open Hannah's bedroom door, unsure of who or what I was going to face.

But thankfully Hannah was alone. Her face was damp with sweat and tears as she thrashed around.

She sat bolt upright in bed.

'Get him off me!' she screamed. 'Please don't let him do this.'

It was like she was in a trance. Her eyes were open but I knew that she wasn't really seeing me and her whole body was trembling.

I sat on the bed and grabbed her hands.

'Hannah, it's Maggie,' I told her calmly, gently squeezing her hands. 'You're OK. You're at my house and you're having a bad dream.'

As I repeated this to her, I could slowly see the recognition coming back into her face as she looked around the bedroom.

'He's not here?' she asked, her voice hoarse.

'No, lovey, it was just a nightmare,' I soothed. 'It wasn't real. There's no one here, Hannah, it's only us. You're safe now.'

To be honest, after everything she had been through in the past twenty-four hours, I wasn't surprised that she'd had such a vivid nightmare. She'd spent all day talking about the horrendous things had happened to her in detail so it was no wonder that she was reliving it all again in her sleep.

'It felt so real,' she sighed. 'Lenny was right here in the room and he was attacking me. I was trying to fight him off but he'd pinned me down and I couldn't move. It was horrible, Maggie.'

'I know, lovey,' I told her. 'But it was just a nightmare. Lenny can't hurt you anymore. You're here safe with me.'

'But what if the police don't keep him in prison and he comes looking for me?' she babbled. 'What if he does find me? Or if he can't find me, he might go after Mum and Molly and hurt them because he's angry at me.'

In my experience, children often got like this after they'd given police interviews. They'd finally broken their silence after being too scared to speak up for months or even years, in some cases, and it was natural for a child to panic about their abuser finding out and to think of the worst-case scenarios. I knew all I could do was approach her fears logically and hope that would be enough to reassure her.

'Hannah, you've done the right thing,' I told her. 'No one is going to get you. You're safe here in my house and Lenny and his friends don't know where you are. If they did, I'm in no doubt that they would have come around here by now. And even if someone did know you were here, the house is all locked up so they couldn't get in.'

'But what if they did get in?' she asked, terror etched on her face.

'Then I would grab my mobile phone and call the police straight away and they would be round here in seconds. But Hannah, in reality that's not going to happen.'

I sat with her for a little while longer, answering her questions and giving her as much reassurance as I could.

'It's still the middle of the night and I think we both need to try and get some more sleep,' I told her gently.

'I'm going to leave your bedroom door wide open and I'll do the same with mine too so we'll be able to hear each other, and you can call me whenever you want. I'm going to leave the landing light on too.'

Hannah nodded but she still looked terrified. I wished I

could take her fear and panic away, but I knew that all I could do was to be calm and logical and talk her through it.

The next morning, I threw myself into organisational mode. Hannah was still completely shell-shocked and she was very quiet. I could see she was drained by everything that had happened at the police station and a disturbed night of sleep. I rang her school and spoke to Mr Granger.

'I'm afraid Hannah won't be back,' I told him. 'We're going to have to pull her out of school for the time being.'

I explained that I couldn't disclose confidential information to him, but that Hannah had been caught up a situation with an older man and the police were now involved.

'I'm so sorry to hear that, that's terrible,' he replied. 'She's only been here a few months but she's a smart girl.'

I explained the local authority were going to look into sorting out a tutor but it normally took several weeks.

'I'll go and talk to her teachers and get a folder of work and some textbooks together so she can keep up with her studies in the meantime,' he told me.

I also phoned Emma to see if there was any update from the police, but she hadn't heard anything. She had managed to organise another contact session with Shelley and Molly after Molly finished school, which seemed to cheer Hannah up.

That afternoon, we drove back to Social Services. Shelley and Molly had already arrived and were waiting in reception with Emma.

Shelley beamed and gave Hannah a hug, but Molly hung back.

'Hi Mol,' said Hannah tentatively, smiling at her little sister. 'You've had your hair cut. It looks really nice. You look so grown up.'

Molly looked at the ground and didn't say a word to her.

I could see the look of shame on Hannah's face when she saw that the plaster was still on her sister's arm.

'Maggie and I will show you to the contact room and then we'll leave you to it,' Emma told them.

As we walked down the corridor, Hannah hung back to walk alongside Molly.

'Did Mum talk to you and explain what had happened to me?' she asked her nervously. 'Did she tell you why I couldn't see you?'

Molly refused to meet Hannah's eye as we went into the contact room.

'She said you knew who pushed me over,' she replied, her voice strained.

'I don't know who did it, but I know they did it to get at me,' Hannah nodded.

'So it *was* your fault,' Molly snapped angrily. 'You let them do this to me. How could you let them hurt me? You're my big sister, you're supposed to protect me.'

Hannah burst into tears.

'No Mol, I didn't. It was the opposite. I didn't want them to hurt you. That's why I said I didn't want to see you and Mum anymore. That's the only way I knew I could keep you safe. Lenny could do whatever he wanted to me but not to you.'

'I don't care,' yelled Molly. 'I hate you and everything you've done to Mum and me.'

With that, she stormed out of the contact room and stomped off down the corridor.

Emma and I exchanged glances.

'It's OK, I'll go and talk to her,' said Shelley.

Hannah was inconsolable.

'She hates me, Maggie,' she wept.

'She'll come around but it's going to take her a bit of time,' I told her gently. 'She's had months of worrying about you and then she thought you didn't want to see her anymore. It's a lot for all of you to take in.'

Ten minutes later, Shelley and Molly came back in. Molly was very subdued and sat there in silence, her face sullen, while Hannah and her mum chatted. Things seemed amicable enough, so Emma and I left them to it and went into another office for a chat.

'As well as counselling for Hannah, I think it would be a good idea to try and get them some family therapy,' I told her once we were by ourselves.

'It's not just Hannah who needs help, they all do. Molly is only thirteen and you can see there's a lot of hurt there.'

Emma agreed, but sadly we both knew the reality – there were so few resources for counselling and demand was so high they could be on a waiting list for months.

'One of the social workers here has just done some family counselling training,' said Emma. 'So perhaps she could do some sessions with the three of them in the meantime?'

While it wasn't therapy, it would give them an opportunity to talk things through in a safe environment with someone there to steer them.

Hannah's actions had had a deep impact on Molly. She'd suffered months of anxiety when Hannah had disappeared at night and not come home, coupled with the hurt of feeling rejected by her beloved older sister. I knew it could take a long time for those wounds to start to heal, and I just hoped that the sisters would be able to repair their damaged relationship.

When they came out of the contact room an hour later, Molly still looked subdued.

Shelley gave Hannah a hug but Molly walked off down the corridor abruptly without saying goodbye.

'She just needs a little bit of time,' Shelley reassured Hannah.

At least they had all managed to be in the same room together for an hour.

Hannah was downcast on the way home.

'Do you think Molly's ever going to forgive me, Maggie?' she asked, her forehead creased.

'She's only thirteen,' I told her. 'It's a lot for her to take in. She's still hurting about everything that's happened but I'm sure she'll come around in time.'

Sadly, I knew there was no quick fix. It was going to take months for the family to try to get over the hurt and pain of everything that had happened.

At ten o'clock that night, Hannah had just gone to bed when my phone rang. I saw Shelley's name flash up on the screen and I answered, assuming that she was ringing to talk through today's contact session and how it had gone. But when I picked it up, there was pandemonium. I could hear Molly screaming in the background.

'Maggie, someone's just put a brick through our front window,' Shelley gasped, sounding frantic. 'There's glass everywhere. What if it's him? What if it's Lenny come to teach us a lesson to get back at Hannah? I don't know what to do, Maggie. Molly's hysterical and I'm too scared to go outside and see if there's anyone there.'

'Ring the police,' I urged. 'Try and stay calm and tell them what's happened. Is there a neighbour you can call who can go and check outside for you?'

'Yes,' she said shakily. 'I'll do that.'

'OK,' I told her. 'Then ring me back so I know you're both safe.'

As I put the phone down, I saw Hannah at the top of the stairs in her pyjamas looking anxious.

'Was that my mum?' she asked. 'What's happened?'

I couldn't lie to her.

'Yes, lovey. They're OK, but someone has just put a brick through their front window,' I explained.

Hannah sunk down to the floor and started to cry.

'It's OK, Hannah,' I told her gently. 'Your mum is going to ring the police and a neighbour's going to check there's no one outside. It's probably just silly teenagers messing about and they'll have run off by now.'

Hannah shook her head.

'It's him, I know it is,' she sobbed. 'He's gone over there to hurt them like he said he would if I ever told anyone.

'He's going to kill them and it's going to be all my fault.'

I wrapped my arms around her and prayed to God that she was wrong.

FOURTEEN

Taking the Blame

Hannah paced up and down the kitchen floor in her pyjamas.

'Please ring my mum back,' she begged me. 'Please ring her back and check they're OK.'

I tried calling Shelley but it went straight to voicemail. Hannah was getting more and more hysterical by the minute.

'She will probably be on the phone to a neighbour or to the police,' I reassured her.

'But what if she's not?' worried Hannah. 'What if they're hurt or someone's got into the house?'

Five minutes later Shelley called back and I pounced on the phone.

'Are you OK?' I asked her. 'Were either of you hurt?'

'We're fine,' she sighed, sounding exhausted. 'Molly's a bit upset, but we're more shaken up than anything. Luckily Molly was in bed and I was in the kitchen making a cup of tea when it happened.'

She had called the police to report it and a couple of

neighbours had checked the whole house and the garden but there was no sign of anyone.

'I just need to clean up all the glass now,' she said. 'Although I want the police to see it first.'

They'd said it could be a couple of hours before they were able to send someone round.

'Do you think it was connected to Hannah, Maggie?' she asked, sounding worried.

'It's impossible to say,' I sighed. 'I know we're all very jumpy at the minute but it's probably just a stupid teenage prank.' I knew I was clutching at straws. 'Has it happened to any other houses in the street?'

'Not that I can see,' she told me.

I could see Hannah was desperate to speak to her mum so I handed her the phone.

'Mum, I'm so sorry,' she told her. 'It's all my fault. Tell Molly I'm sorry too.'

By the time Hannah hung up, she was angry.

'Why won't the police do anything?' she ranted. 'Can't they get someone to guard the house or give them a special alarm?'

'I'm afraid it's not like it is on TV, lovey,' I told her. 'The police just don't have the resources.

'I think if they genuinely thought there was evidence that your mum and Molly were at risk then they would step in to protect them, but we don't have any proof that this was anything more than a prank. I know you're worried about Lenny, but we don't know for certain that it was him who did this.

'I'm going to phone Emma for an update tomorrow, so I'll talk to her about it then.'

Eventually, I managed to persuade Hannah back to bed, before turning in myself. Although we knew Shelley and Molly were OK, I don't think either of us got much sleep that night. I tossed and turned, and I heard Hannah getting up a few times to go to the bathroom.

For the past few days, we'd been pretty much cooped up indoors so when we woke up the next day to a sunny, clear morning, I was determined to get us outside.

'We need some bread and milk, so we're going to go out,' I told Hannah after breakfast, grabbing my car keys.

'But why?' she asked, her eyes wide with fear. 'We don't really need milk or bread. Or maybe Louisa could bring some to us? I bet she wouldn't mind.'

'I know you're nervous, but we can't stay cooped up in the house forever,' I told her. 'We have to try and live our lives.'

But Hannah didn't look convinced. She just looked terrified.

I was going to drive us to a nearby village so we could have a walk around and get some fresh air. Hannah took ages to put her trainers on but eventually we made it.

'It's really pretty here,' I told her as I pulled up into a car park. 'There are some nice shops that we can look at.'

As we walked down the main street, the pavement was so narrow we had to walk in single file. I was chatting away to Hannah but she wasn't saying a word. I turned around to see if she was OK, but to my surprise, she had stopped a little way behind me and was doubled over on the pavement. I ran back to her.

'What's wrong, lovey?' I asked her.

'We need to go back to the car,' she mumbled. 'We need to go back to the car now, Maggie.'

'Why flower?' I asked, confused.

'We just do,' she insisted, and I could hear the urgency in her voice.

She looked ashen and beads of sweat were dripping down her forehead.

'I can't breathe, Maggie,' she gasped, holding onto my arm with a vice-like grip. 'I think I'm having a heart attack.'

'Goodness, you're shaking like a leaf,' I replied.

I knew instinctively that she was having a panic attack and I needed to get her back to the car as soon as possible.

'Come on, let's walk back to the car park,' I told her gently. 'Put one foot in front of the other.'

Hannah was very shaky and was still gasping for breath and clinging tightly to my arm as we walked along.

'Good girl,' I soothed. 'We're nearly there now . . . You can do this.'

When we got to the car, I guided her round to the front passenger door and she collapsed onto the seat.

'Lock the doors, Maggie,' she panted. 'Lock the doors now.'

I did as she'd asked.

It was a warm day but Hannah was still shaking so I reached into the back of the car for the blanket that I kept there and wrapped it around her shoulders. It was soft and furry and feeling something tactile against their skin often helped calm children down.

'I can't still breathe,' she gasped. 'I think I'm dying, Maggie.'

I held her hand and felt how hot and clammy it was.

'Close your eyes and listen to my voice,' I told her calmly. 'Now take a big deep breath in through your nose and then blow it out through your mouth.'

I did it along with her.

'Good girl,' I said. 'Now let's do it again. Breathe in and breathe out. And again.'

As she breathed in and out, I patted her hand rhythmically.

'My heart's going to explode,' she panicked. 'Maggie, you need to call an ambulance.'

'You're OK,' I reassured her. 'Just keep on breathing, Hannah, it's going to be fine.'

We sat there in the car as I slowly and calmly guided her through her breathing.

When I could see that she'd started to calm down, I rummaged in the glove compartment and found a packet of extra strong mints.

'Have one of these,' I said, offering her one.

When people felt like they'd lost control, as they did when they were having a panic attack, there were a number of techniques I used that helped to ground them and bring them out of their state of panic. Things they could touch, like the snuggly blanket or taste or smell, would help. I hoped sucking on the mint and focusing on its strong flavour would help to distract her, calm her down and bring her back into the moment.

Thankfully, it seemed to work, and gradually Hannah's breathing started to regulate. She sagged down in the front seat, pale and limp, looking exhausted.

'What happened, flower?' I asked her. 'What made you react like that?'

'I saw him,' she told me, her eyes wide with fear.

'You saw Lenny?' I asked, feeling my heart starting to pound. Surely he couldn't have found us here, of all places?

'It was his car,' she told me breathlessly. 'I saw a silver Mazda just like his driving on the road right next to us. I'm sure it was him, Maggie.'

'Sweetheart, there are a lot of silver cars on the road,' I told her, sighing inwardly with relief. 'It doesn't mean it was Lenny's. Do you know his registration number?' I asked.

She shook her head.

'There you go,' I said. 'It could have been anyone's. But if it makes you feel better, as soon as we get home I'll give Emma a ring and I'll see if there's any update from the police, OK?'

Hannah nodded.

She was still a bit shaky after her panic attack so when we got home, Hannah lay down on the sofa and I put a film on for her. Meanwhile, I went upstairs and called Emma.

'Maggie, I was just about to ring you,' she told me. 'Could I pop round and have a chat to you?'

There was something about the tone of her voice that stopped me in my tracks.

'What is it?' I asked warily. 'What's happened?'

'Let's talk when I come round,' she replied firmly. 'I can come over now if that works?'

I felt a growing sense of unease, but agreed, and within fifteen minutes, Emma was standing on the doorstep.

'Do you want Hannah to join us as well?' I asked, once I'd let her inside, but Emma shook her head.

'It would be better if you and I had a conversation first,' she told me.

We went into the kitchen where I made us both a coffee and we sat down at the table.

'PC Williams called me this morning,' she said. 'I'm afraid it's not good news, Maggie.'

She explained that Lenny had been arrested and interviewed. He'd been held for as long as they were legally allowed, but he'd eventually been released without charge.

'How come?' I gasped. 'After everything that he's put Hannah through. He drugged and raped her, for God's sake.'

Emma shrugged her shoulders.

'PC Williams was as frustrated as we are, but the Crown Prosecution Service didn't feel there was enough to secure a prosecution,' she told me. 'There's no DNA evidence to prove that she was raped, and it's Hannah's word against his.'

'But he groomed her, won her trust and abused her in the most despicable way. She's just a child, Emma.'

'I know,' she told me. 'And he's a twenty-four-year-old man. I'm as angry and upset as you are, Maggie.'

My heart sank. I knew he was older, but I'd never imagined that there was an age gap of nearly ten years. At twenty-four, he was a fully grown man.

Emma explained that Lenny had admitted knowing Hannah and starting a relationship with her. He claimed that Hannah had told him she was seventeen, and when he had found out her real age, he'd broken things off. He'd denied having any kind of sexual relationship with her and claimed that Hannah had made up everything because she was upset that he'd finished with her.

'But what about the drugs?' I asked, infuriated. 'What about the fact that he forced her to get on trains and deliver packages to other places for him?'

They had searched Lenny's flat but there had been no drugs found and no evidence of dealing.

'He must have known that Hannah had gone to the police when she disappeared with the drugs and the money and stopped answering her phone,' I sighed. 'He's not stupid. He would have quickly got rid of anything that could convict him.

'But what about the messages on Hannah's phone?' I asked suddenly, feeling a new surge of hope.

'Again, he was very careful not to talk about packages or anything incriminating on those,' replied Emma. 'It's all train times and meeting places. There are a few abusive messages, but even so, ultimately the police can't prove that it was him messaging Hannah.

'He never used his name on the messages and they never found the phone that those messages were sent from when they searched his flat.'

This guy wasn't stupid. I knew it would have been a pay-as-you-go untraceable 'burner' phone that he would have just destroyed.

'In the CPS's eyes, it's just not enough, Maggie,' sighed Emma. 'If it's any consolation, the police have said they're going to be keeping a close eye on him and his movements.'

'Oh, I've no doubt that he'll be watching his back after this,' I said. 'He knows they're onto him, so he'll have to lay low for a while.'

I was absolutely gutted at the news, but more than anything, I was devastated for Hannah. She'd bared her soul to us and now no one was going to be punished for hurting and exploiting her.

'I'm afraid it gets worse, Maggie,' Emma told me, looking upset.

I didn't see how it could get any worse.

'The only thing the police *can* prove is that Hannah was in possession of a fairly large quantity of a class A drug, which means that they're going to charge her with possession.'

'What?' I gasped.

I couldn't believe what I was hearing.

'If Hannah admits it, they'll issue her with a caution, but if she doesn't, she'll be charged with possession with intent to supply. If that happens, then it's likely it will have to be dealt with by the youth courts.'

'But she was forced into it,' I exclaimed. 'She was groomed and raped and abused. She didn't even know what was in those packages.'

'Absolutely,' agreed Emma. 'I'm as horrified as you are. But I spoke to the duty solicitor at Social Services before I came here and she feels that it's in Hannah's interests to admit the charge and take the caution. Even though there are mitigating circumstances, she doesn't feel it's worth the risk or the stress of going to court.'

I was horrified that Hannah was the one being punished while the real criminal was walking round scot-free. It was unbelievably unfair.

A caution wasn't a conviction, but it would stay on Hannah's criminal record forever and it could affect her job prospects in the future.

The worst thing about all of this was that we were now going to have to break the news to Hannah.

'How on earth are we going to tell her?' I sighed, feeling sick to my stomach. 'It's going to tip her over the edge. She's having nightmares and panic attacks about Lenny, and now we have to tell her that not only is he free to walk the streets but she's the one who's going to be punished. What kind of justice is that?'

I'd been constantly reassuring her and telling her that the police would sort it all out and keep her safe. Although this was beyond my control, I felt as though I had personally failed her.

'I'll talk to her,' Emma promised. 'They want her to come down to the station at ten o'clock tomorrow morning so they can issue the caution.'

I was at a loss and had no idea what to do. How was I going to make Hannah feel safe after this? And how was I going to reassure Shelley and Molly that they weren't at risk from Lenny?

As we walked into the living room and sat down, I felt devastated. The system had let Hannah down. We'd all let her down and I felt responsible.

She could immediately tell from the expression on my face that something was wrong.

'What is it?' she asked, sitting up on the sofa. 'Has something happened to Mum and Molly?'

'Your mum and Molly are fine, flower,' I told her, switching off the TV. 'Emma wants to talk to you about the police.'

It took all my strength to hold back the tears as I saw the look of utter despair on Hannah's face as Emma repeated what she'd told me.

'But he hurt *me*,' she sobbed. 'Lenny forced me to deliver those drugs. He didn't give me a choice. He tricked me. He pretended he was my boyfriend and did what he wanted with me but they're not going to send him to prison. It's so unfair,' she sobbed.

'I know it is, lovey,' I said. 'I completely agree with you.'

'You told me the police would keep us safe, Maggie, and that I had to tell them so they could make sure he couldn't do it to anyone else.'

'I know, Hannah,' I sighed. 'And I'm so sorry it hasn't turned out that way.'

'Why don't they believe me?' she cried. 'Why would I make up such horrible things?'

'It's not that they don't believe you, sweetie. Everyone believes you but the police don't have enough evidence to guarantee that if they take the case to court, he'll be found guilty.'

I could see all our words and explanations were meaningless. In Hannah's eyes, she'd told the truth, and no one had listened.

Before Emma left, she let me know that she had already called Shelley and told her the news.

'How did she take it?' I asked.

'As you can imagine,' shrugged Emma. 'She was absolutely devastated and furious.'

Unfortunately, Shelly had had too much time off work and wasn't able to get cover for her nursing shift in time to be able to take Hannah to the police station the following morning.

'I'll take her,' I said.

After Emma had left, Hannah was very tearful. Understandably she was distraught and absolutely terrified about what was going to happen to her at the police station. I gently talked her through what it would involve.

I'd taken children to be cautioned before and it wasn't a nice experience, so I wanted her to be prepared.

'It's likely that they will be very stern and serious,' I told her. 'When they talk to you about it, you've got to put everything else out of your head and remember that they're just talking about the drugs.

'They're not talking about whether they believe you about Lenny and how you got hold of the drugs. They're just talking about the fact that those drugs were found in your possession.

'I know it's hard, Hannah, but you have to accept this and not argue against them, otherwise they might decide to deal with you in the youth court.'

She nodded but I could see that she was dreading it. I think we both were.

The next morning, we walked into the police station at 10 a.m. on the dot.

'Someone will take you through in a minute,' the receptionist told us.

There was no sign of PC Williams this time. A male PC came out and led us to a side room that was filled with shelves of dusty box files. There was no introduction or niceties.

'I need to take your fingerprints,' he told Hannah gruffly. 'They will be kept on our system so we'll know if you reoffend in the future.'

Hannah looked terrified as he patted each of her fingers in an inkpad and pressed them onto paper. Afterwards he took us to an office.

'Stand over there,' he told Hannah. 'An inspector will be down to see you shortly.'

Hannah turned around and looked at me for reassurance.

'You're doing well,' I whispered. 'It will be OK.'

The inspector, a grey-haired man in his fifties, came striding in with a serious look on his face. He made Hannah stand in front of his desk and from where I was standing, by the door at the back of the room, I could see that she was shaking. He looked at the papers on his desk and then stared at her with an unwavering gaze.

'Hannah Dougan, you are being issued this youth caution for being in possession of a class A drug,' he said in a loud, stern voice.

'A youth caution is a serious matter and a record of it will be kept by police. In this situation, because of mitigating circumstances, we don't feel that an intervention programme is appropriate, as there's a low risk of you reoffending.

'But if you do reoffend in the next twelve months, then we will have no hesitation in sending you to be dealt with by the youth courts.'

He paused.

'Do you understand?' he asked Hannah.

She nodded silently, tears streaming down her face.

Then he gave her a form, confirming that she consented to receiving a caution, which she signed with trembling hands.

'Your appropriate adult will need to sign it too,' he said, looking to me at the back of the room.

As I signed it, I realised my hands were shaking too.

'You can leave now,' he told her. 'And I hope we don't ever have to see you here again, Hannah.'

I hoped so too. The whole thing seemed so unjust and unfair and I could see how shaken up Hannah was.

She was the victim here, and yet she had been punished and treated like a criminal. Meanwhile, the real criminal was walking the streets plotting his next move. And until he was safely locked up behind bars, I knew none of us were going to rest.

FIFTEEN

Sanctuary by the Sea

The incessant ringing of the smoke alarm echoed loudly throughout the house and sent me into a panic. I bolted downstairs to the kitchen where the smell of burning was coming from. To my surprise, all I found were two singed slices of toast in the toaster and Hannah in floods of tears.

'Hey, what's happened?' I asked gently. 'You can't be crying about burnt toast?'

But she was sobbing so much she couldn't speak.

I sat her down at the kitchen table then opened the patio doors to let out the acrid smoke.

'Let's start again, shall we?' I smiled.

I made her two new slices of toast and a cup of tea and joined her at the table.

'So, what's all this really about?' I asked. 'I'm famous for my toast burning in this house and that bloomin' smoke alarm is always going off, so don't you worry about any of that.'

Hannah gave me a weak smile.

'So, what is it?' I asked. 'I know this isn't about toast so what's really upsetting you, Hannah?'

She fiddled with a slice of toast for a moment before looking up at me, her blue eyes filled with tears.

'Nothing feels fair anymore,' she sighed. 'No one believes me about what happened, and Lenny has got away with everything. He's not got into trouble and I have. How is that right?'

Hannah had been very tearful in the days following her trip to the police station to be cautioned. She was regularly having nightmares too, so she had dark shadows under her eyes.

'I completely agree with you,' I nodded. 'What happened to you isn't fair, and I'm angry and upset as well.'

I put my arm around her.

'I know it doesn't feel like it at the moment, but things will get better, lovey,' I reassured her. 'All we can do is try to focus on the positives and the main thing is, you're safe now. You're free to live your life away from Lenny now. Everyone knows what he's done and we won't ever let him hurt you again. OK?'

Hannah nodded but I knew it wasn't going to be an easy road.

With Lenny walking away unpunished, there was no sense of relief that her ordeal was over. Without any sense of closure or justice, I knew it would be incredibly hard for her to draw a line under it and move on with the rest of her life.

Hannah was also reluctant to leave the house – in fact, it took all of my coaxing to even get her to come out of her room. A tutor was now coming twice a week for a couple of hours, so she wasn't even leaving the house to go to school. I had suggested we both go swimming or to the shops to persuade her to get out and about, but she wasn't keen. Because of what had happened with Lenny, she'd gradually lost touch with all of her school friends and had become incredibly isolated from her peers. Wracking my brains in an effort to try and persuade her to leave the house, I asked her if she wanted to go to the cinema with Molly. Even though I would drop her off and pick her up, I wanted to try and encourage little bits of independence again. But as with everything else I'd suggested, she flatly refused.

While she was being tutored one day, Becky came round to the house for a supervision session. It was a chance for me to talk through what was happening, how I was feeling and get any help and support that I might need to deal with the situation.

'So, how's Hannah?' she asked me.

'Up and down,' I told her. 'She's still suffering from nightmares and panic attacks and she's been crying a lot. Understandably, in the aftermath of everything with the police, she's really struggling with the idea that no one believes her.'

'Hopefully counselling will help her come to terms with some of that,' said Becky. 'It's really hard, but in time, hopefully Hannah can learn to move past what happened to her.

'And how are you?' she asked.

I shrugged.

'I just have this overwhelming feeling that I've let her down,' I sighed.

'Maggie, the system has let her down, not you,' Becky told me firmly. 'Unfortunately, the reality is, things don't always work out the way we want them to and we're bound by the constraints of the legal system. You and Emma have done the very best you can for her.'

'I just don't know how to help her,' I replied.

'All you can do is be there for her, listen when she wants to talk and that will help her process things.'

I still had waves of anger and frustration that Lenny wasn't going to be prosecuted. I knew that if I was finding it hard to deal with, it must have been unbearable for Hannah.

Becky and I also talked about Hannah's Looked After Child (LAC) review, which had been scheduled for later that week. It was a meeting where all of the people involved in Hannah's care would get together to come up with a long-term plan for her future.

'What are your feelings about what's best for her in the long run?' asked Becky.

'I know that she needs to get back into some sort of routine and go back to regular schooling again,' I said. 'Where and how that can happen because of all the safety concerns, I don't know.'

That same evening Shelley rang me. She and Hannah were in regular contact now and phoned and texted in between contact sessions.

'How are you doing?' I asked her.

'Is Hannah around?' she said. 'I don't want her to know that I'm calling you.'

'No, she's upstairs in her bedroom getting ready for bed,' I told her. 'What is it, Shelley? Is everything OK?'

'Not really,' she replied. 'Someone has just tried to break into the house.'

She was very calm, but I could hear that her voice was shaking.

'A neighbour saw a man on the flat roof at the back trying to get in Molly's bedroom window. He banged on the window and the guy ran off. The neighbour didn't see his face properly because he had a hoodie on.'

I felt sick to my stomach. I knew I was thinking the same as Shelley. What if this was Lenny or one of his associates? Were they ever going to leave Hannah and her family alone? How long would it be before they managed to find out this address?

'Did you call the police?' I asked her.

'Yes, they're on their way round now,' she said. 'But to be honest, I'm not sure there's much they can do.'

This time Shelley wasn't hysterical. She just sounded weary.

'We can't stay here tonight,' she told me. 'Molly's terrified and there's no way we'd get any sleep after what's happened, so we're going to my friend's house.'

'I understand,' I told her.

'It's the same old story, Maggie,' she sighed. 'There's no evidence that this is connected to Hannah but it's too much of a coincidence that all these horrible things keep happening to us. There's no proof and so the police can't seem to do anything.'

I knew I'd be thinking exactly the same thing if I was in her situation, and once again, I felt a wave of helplessness at everything that was happening.

'We can talk things through at the LAC review later this week,' I promised her.

With the LAC review just around the corner, I knew I also needed to check with Hannah if she wanted to come along.

'What is it?' she asked, sounding puzzled when I mentioned it to her.

'It's a meeting to talk about what's happened and where we go from here. Me, your mum and Emma will be there, as well as my supervising social worker, Becky.'

Hannah wrinkled her nose.

'I don't want to,' she sighed. 'It's weird if everyone's talking about me while I'm just sat there.'

The review was being held at Social Services, so on the day, I arranged for Hannah to wait in one of the contact rooms. That way, if she did change her mind, she could always join us. Once she'd said hello to her mum, I settled her into the room with some schoolwork.

'So how are things, Shelley?' Emma asked, as she carried a tray of teas and coffees into the meeting room.

'Not great,' she sighed. 'The attempted break-in the other night really shook me and Molly up. We couldn't stay at my mate's forever, so we've had to go back home, but neither of us are sleeping properly and poor Molly's so tired she's been falling asleep at school.'

She paused.

'So, I've made a decision,' she said at last. 'The bottom line is, we can't live like this anymore. After everything that's happened and because we know that monster who hurt Hannah is still out there somewhere, I don't think any of us are ever going to feel safe again. I've thought long and hard about it, and I've realised that our only option is to move. I've given the housing association notice on the house.'

'Well if you're struggling to find somewhere and it would help, I can have a chat with the council,' suggested Emma. 'Social Services can write a letter of support to say that you need priority housing.'

Shelley shook her head.

'We need to go somewhere much further afield,' she explained. 'I think we need to get out of the area completely and have a fresh start altogether. My brother's in Devon, and I've decided that it might be nice to move down there so we can be near him.'

'Wow,' I gasped, shocked at this new revelation. 'Devon is a long way away.'

'There is one thing that I need to check before I do any of this, though,' Shelley went on, a worried look flashing across her face.

'I'm not willing to go anywhere without Hannah,' she said firmly. 'She's been through so much and she needs this fresh start more than any of us.

'So, what I really wanted to ask you all was whether Hannah would be able to leave care now and come with us?'

She looked nervously at Emma for an answer, who looked as shocked as I felt, but she quickly recovered herself.

'As you know, Hannah came into care under a Section 20, which means it was voluntary,' explained Emma. 'You've still got parental responsibility for her, so it means that you can take her out of care at any point.

'If Social Services have concerns then we can object but if you're moving out of the area and there's no threat to Hannah's safety, then I think we would all support you in this.'

I nodded in agreement.

'So we could really do this?' gasped Shelley. 'We could all move together?'

'Yes,' laughed Emma.

'And are you OK with that, Maggie?' Shelley asked me.

'If Hannah's happy, then that's good enough for me,' I told her, smiling. 'Remember, your parenting was never being called into question, Shelley. We can all see that you're a good mum and you love your daughter and want the best for her.'

Of course, I was going to be sad to see Hannah go, but after everything that had happened, it was clear that she needed some normality and to get back to full-time schooling. I agreed with Shelley that she would be much safer and happier doing that in a completely different area.

'Have you mentioned this to Hannah?' I asked Shelley.

'No, it's something I've only just decided on myself, so I wanted to check that I was allowed to do it first before I told the girls,' she explained.

'How quickly are you thinking of moving?' asked Emma.

'Honestly, it would be great to move as soon as we can,' replied Shelley. 'I'd like to get the girls settled into schools and just get away from here and start to put all this behind us. We can stay with my brother until we find a house.'

We were all agreed that this was the best way forward. It could happen as quickly as Shelley wanted it to as Hannah wasn't a small child who needed to go through a settling-in process to get her used to living with her birth family again.

'Obviously, I'd like to have a word with Hannah about it and make sure that she's happy with it too,' Emma told Shelley.

It was a big life change for the whole family, and after everything else that had happened, it wasn't something we could just spring on Hannah today at Social Services. I knew Emma would want to talk to her in the familiar, safe environment of my house and gauge Hannah's response. If Shelley was the one to tell her, Hannah might feel as if she had no choice but to agree with her mum.

Emma came round to see Hannah the following day.

'At the meeting yesterday, your mum was talking about the future. After everything that's happened here, she thinks it might be better to make a fresh start somewhere else. She's been thinking about moving to Devon to be closer to your uncle, and we wondered how you would feel about that?'

Hannah's face fell and she looked like she was about to burst into tears.

'But that's miles away,' she exclaimed. 'We couldn't do contact then. How would I see her and Molly if they lived there?'

'No, sorry Hannah, I didn't explain that very well.' Emma smiled apologetically. 'What I meant was, how would you feel about moving to Devon with them and making a new life there with your mum and Molly?'

Hannah looked stunned.

'What?' she gasped. 'I'm allowed to go too?'

'Yes,' Emma laughed. 'Of course you are. Maggie and I actually think it would be a really positive move for you to move out of this area. You'd be able to start afresh and go to a new school and meet new people. It's going to be a big change for you all and it will be hard, but it might also help you to move forward.

'Obviously our main priority is for you to be happy though, Hannah, so we wanted to see how you felt about it first.'

'Yes!' she gasped, her eyes wide. 'I want to do it. I want to be with my mum and Molly and for everything to go back to how it was before I met Lenny.'

It was wonderful to see her looking excited and positive about something again.

'Your mum will be so pleased,' I smiled at her. 'She was really worried about what you were going to say, and she wasn't prepared to do the move without you.'

'Can I phone her?' asked Hannah, practically bouncing in her seat with excitement. 'Can I ring her, Maggie, and tell her that I really want to come?'

'Go ahead,' I smiled.

Emma and I watched as Hannah picked up her mobile, pacing up and down impatiently while it rang.

'Emma just told me about Devon,' she gasped when Shelley answered. 'I'm so happy, Mum.'

They talked for a few minutes, then Shelley must have asked to speak to me as Hannah passed me the phone. I could hear Shelley was in tears.

'I'm so, so pleased,' she sniffed. 'I felt sick thinking about it because I was so worried she wasn't going to like the idea.'

'Well as you can tell, she's very happy,' I told her, smiling as I looked over at Hannah.

I knew it was a huge relief for all of them.

A few days later, Shelley took Molly and Hannah to Devon for a couple of nights to check out the schools and look around the area, as they hadn't been for a couple of years. I could see Hannah was filled with a mixture of nerves and excitement.

'I'm sure you'll love it,' I reassured her the night before she left. 'Although it's going to be very strange here without you.'

It was the first day that I'd had entirely to myself since Hannah had come to live with me four months ago. It was a treat to have a day free, and I'd arranged to have lunch with Graham, who I'd only seen a handful of times recently. We had a lovely time catching up, and then after lunch I went to see Liz and Martin. I'd had the odd text from them saying things were going well but I was desperate to see Albie and Ethan.

When I knocked on the door of the flat, the twins both came running to open it.

'Hello boys,' I grinned, as they hurled themselves at me excitedly.

'Come on in,' grinned Martin from behind them.

Liz looked tired, but she seemed happy and relaxed and was sitting on the floor building train tracks with the boys.

'Wow, you two have grown so much,' I told them. 'Soon you'll be taller than me.'

As usual, Albie was the more talkative of the pair and Ethan the more serious, thoughtful one. They showed me how well they could read their Biff and Chip books from school, pictures they'd drawn and how much they loved Lego Star Wars – even as much as Manchester United.

'Have you got a house full of children now the boys have left?' Liz asked as we caught up.

'Just the one,' I told them. 'I've still got Hannah. That was the girl who came to me just before the twins came home.'

'I bet it's been easy with just the one,' said Martin. 'It'll have been a lot quieter than having these two around.'

If only you knew the truth, I thought to myself. The last few months had been anything but quiet.

As I gave the boys a hug goodbye, it felt like a weight had been lifted.

It had been a lovely, carefree day that had taken me away from the intense events of the past few months. I'd spent a lot of one-on-one time with Hannah and it was nice for me to get out of the house and talk to other people.

But, after she'd been gone for a couple of nights, I was anxious to see her. I was praying the trip had gone well as I drove to pick her up from the station.

Hannah, Shelley and Molly were waiting for me outside.

'So how was Devon?' I asked, smiling at them.

'It was cool,' Hannah said excitedly. 'I loved being near the sea and seeing my cousins. The school was big, but I think it will be OK.'

I had a quick word with Shelley too.

'I just want to get on with it now, Maggie,' she told me. 'It feels like we're in a state of limbo here and it was so nice for Hannah to walk around and not be scared or worried about who she's going to see. It's the fresh start we all need.'

It was clear that the visit had made Shelley more keen to leave than ever. She explained that they were going to stay with her brother whilst they looked for somewhere to live, and Shelley was going to get some nursing shifts through an agency.

'If I can sort out the house and pack up everything, I'm hoping that we can leave in just over a week.'

It was quick but I could see it was the right thing for them to do.

A week later and Shelley had sprung into action to make her plan happen. She'd left work, the house was packed up and she had hired a van to drive her and Molly and their things to Devon. Hannah was going to leave the following morning with Emma, who had offered to drive her there. Even though Hannah was moving out of the area, Emma would still be her social worker. There would have to be some follow-ups to check that Hannah was settling in OK. Emma wanted to go to Devon and talk to Hannah's new school and make sure that she was on a waiting list for some counselling. Then she would go and visit them again after six weeks to check how they were getting on.

This wasn't the time for big goodbyes, but it still felt important to mark the end of Hannah's time with me. Everyone was still nervous about Molly and Shelley coming round to my house, so the night before they left, Hannah and I met them for tea at TGI Fridays.

'Are you all set?' I asked Shelley.

'I just want to get there now,' she nodded. 'This will be a new life for us all and a chance to rebuild things. I would never have chosen it before all of this happened, but perhaps it will work out for the best.'

'I'm sure it will,' I smiled. 'And the best thing is, you're doing it together.'

They all seemed excited about it, even though the decision to move had been forced on them.

Shelley had bought me a bunch of flowers and a box of chocolates.

'Thank you for everything, Maggie,' she said, holding back the tears as we said goodbye. 'This has been the hardest thing we've ever been through as a family and you've been a great support to Hannah. If she'd stayed at home, I know things could have worked out very differently and I'll always be grateful to you.'

'She's a lovely girl and I'm going to miss her,' I told Shelley.

I gave her and Molly a hug and then I took Hannah home to get ready for the morning and for our own goodbye.

When we got home, I helped Hannah pack up the last of her things and I gave her a little goodbye present – a leather-bound book and a fluffy pen.

'Sometimes writing your thoughts and feelings down can help you process them,' I told her.

'Thank you,' she smiled. 'I love it. I'm going to miss you, Maggie,' she went on. 'But being here reminds me of the horrible things that happened so I'm looking forward to getting away.'

'I understand,' I told her. 'I think a fresh start will do you all the world of good.'

After she'd got ready for bed, I knocked on her bedroom door.

'I've just come to say goodnight,' I told her. 'Just think, you'll be at your uncle's house this time tomorrow night.'

She smiled.

I sat down on the floor next to her bed.

'I'm really proud of you, Hannah,' I told her. 'You've been so brave and strong. I know you feel let down after everything that's happened, but what you've got to focus on now is how far you've come. You were caught up in something that was really dangerous and things could have ended up very differently. But you were brave enough to talk to me and tell the police everything that you'd been through.

'You could have left my house, gone with Lenny and been totally submerged in that world but you got out and now you're free. You're free to go and start a new life without him.'

Hannah's eyes filled with tears and she nodded.

'It's also important to remember that you've been through a lot and it's not all magically going to go away just because you're in a different place. There are going to be times when you need a little bit more help and support because of what you've been through, so don't be afraid to ask for it. Your mum understands that, and I will always be here for you.'

'Could I ring you sometimes if I wanted to?' she asked shyly. 'Or text you?'

'Of course,' I told her. 'I know your mum's happy for us to keep in touch. So whenever you need me, you just call, OK?'

Hannah nodded.

As I walked out of the room, I noticed the stuffed toy mouse and the family photo that Shelley had given Hannah to take with her were still on her bedside table.

'Don't forget those,' I told her, putting them on top of the cardboard box.

As I put the photo in with the rest of her stuff, I had one last look at it. A smiling, happy, carefree Hannah stared back at me and all I could hope was that one day she could be that girl again.

Emma arrived early the next morning to collect Hannah. It never did children any favours if I got emotional when they left, so I did my usual trick to stop myself from crying and that was to keep busy. I checked around the house to make sure Hannah had got everything and then I helped Emma put her things into her car.

'Well then,' smiled Emma. 'I think you're all ready to go.'

'Come and give me a hug,' I told Hannah.

I put my arms around her and gave her a goodbye squeeze.

'Enjoy Devon,' I told her. 'And remember what I said last night. You know where I am.'

She nodded.

'Thank you for believing me, Maggie,' she said.

'Hannah, we all believe you,' I reminded her.

When some children move on, it's a celebration. When Albie and Ethan had gone back to their parents, it had really felt like that. But as I waved goodbye to Hannah, my heart felt heavy.

I had arranged a coffee with Vicky later that morning to try and take my mind off Hannah leaving.

'I tried to do my best for her, but it wasn't enough,' I told Vicky sadly as we sat in her living room together.

Hannah had been groomed, raped and made to do terrible things. It made my blood boil to know that the person who had done that to her was still out there living his life, potentially doing the same thing to another young girl.

'It's so frustrating. I know that everybody did all that they could, but we just couldn't give Hannah the ending that she deserved,' I sighed.

'All you can do is focus on the positives, Maggie,' Vicky told me wisely.

So that's what I tried to do. While Hannah started the long journey to Devon, I focused on the fact that her, her mum and Molly had been reunited. They were making a fresh start together as a family. It was a new beginning for all of them and that had to be enough.

Thirteen months later . . .

SIXTEEN

Second Chances

Walking over to the living-room window, I pointed out the trees through the glass.

'Look at the leaves, Phoenix,' I cooed to the eight-week-old baby girl snuggled in my arms. 'Can you see them moving about in the wind?'

Her tiny rosebud mouth gaped open in wonder and she gave me a gummy smile.

I loved having a baby in the house again, especially a newborn. I relished the cuddles, and nothing could beat burying your nose in their fluffy hair and breathing in that sweet, milky smell.

'Has she been OK?' asked her mum Shola as she walked into the living room.

'As good as gold,' I smiled.

'How was your bath, flower?' I asked her.

'So nice,' she sighed. 'I feel a bit more human again.'

She'd had a bad night with Phoenix, who'd been unsettled with colic.

Shola had come to live with me four months ago. When she arrived, she was seventeen years old and twenty-eight weeks pregnant. She'd been neglected by her drug-addicted mother and had spent most of her childhood in and out of the care system. As a teenager, she'd had issues with alcohol, but she'd been clean and sober for the past few years. However, as she was seventeen and alone, Social Services thought she might not be able to cope with the responsibility of a baby.

To my delight though, Shola had been the easiest mother and baby placement that I'd ever had. Despite everyone's concerns, she'd taken to motherhood naturally. She knew how to make a bottle, change a nappy and engage with her daughter. She'd surprised everyone and I was so proud of her.

She was halfway through a parenting assessment, but if things carried on the way they were, I knew that before long she and Phoenix would hopefully be moving into their own place together.

Phoenix squirmed in my arms and started rubbing her eyes.

'I think someone needs a nap,' said Shola, smiling at her little girl. 'I'll go and put her down.'

'Why don't you try and catch up on a bit of sleep while she does?' I suggested.

'Yeah, I think I will,' she replied. 'Thanks, Maggie.'

I gently handed Phoenix to her and she took her upstairs.

It was little things like that that showed me what a competent mum Shola was. She recognised the cues and most of the time she knew exactly what her baby needed.

To be honest, Shola was so capable of looking after Phoenix that, for the most part, it was more like living with a lodger than a foster child. Nevertheless, I was enjoying spending time with them both, and it was a joy to see Shola flourish.

I was just going into the kitchen to make a cup of tea and make the most of the peace and quiet, when my phone rang.

'Maggie, it's Emma,' said a voice. 'You might not remember me. I'm the social worker who placed Hannah with you.'

'Of course I remember you!' I laughed. 'It hasn't been that long, has it?'

'Well, I wasn't sure as it was over a year ago now,' she replied. 'I wondered if it was possible to come round and have a cup of tea with you?' she went on. 'Are you very busy at the moment?'

'I've got a mother and baby placement here, but Shola's out as much as she's in, so whenever suits you.'

'Tomorrow afternoon?' she suggested.

'Great,' I told her. 'See you then.'

I was filled with curiosity about why Emma wanted to see me. I knew Hannah was fine. Although I hadn't seen her since she'd moved to Devon, she texted me regularly and occasionally she rang me. She, Shelley and Molly had settled into life there, and the move away had provided exactly the fresh start they had all needed so desperately.

I suppose I'll find out tomorrow, I thought to myself as I sipped my tea.

The following day, Shola had taken Phoenix into town to meet a friend. I was just catching up on some paperwork when there was a knock at the door.

Emma looked as youthful as ever.

'You've had your hair cut,' I said. 'It looks lovely.'

'Thanks, Maggie,' she smiled. 'It's good to see you.'

I made us both a coffee and we sat at the kitchen table.

'Have you heard from Hannah?' she asked.

'Yes, I've had lots of texts and she's rung me a few times,' I said. 'It sounds like it's going well for them in Devon, although I know she's found it hard at times.'

She had called me a couple of times when she was struggling with situations at school and she didn't want to worry Shelley.

'I went down to see them four months ago, but I haven't heard anything since,' replied Emma.

She took a sip of her coffee and I looked at her expectantly, wondering when she was going to get to the point and tell me why she'd come over.

'Actually, Hannah's the reason I wanted to speak to you today,' she told me.

I listened intently as she began to talk.

'PC Williams called me the other day,' she began. 'She's actually a detective constable now and she's based in CID at a station in another borough. She wanted to talk to me about a case that she's been working on.'

Emma explained how the police officer had been investigating the case of a fourteen-year-old girl who had been beaten up and raped in some woodland. A passer-by had heard her screaming and called the police.

'When she interviewed the girl, a much more complicated picture emerged,' Emma went on.

It transpired that the girl was from a local children's home. She and her friend had been groomed by an older man they had met at the local shops.

'He bought them expensive presents and took them out in his car,' she told me. 'They were flattered by his attention, and he was kind to them, so it wasn't long before it escalated to going round to parties at his flat, where him and his mates had plied them with drink and drugs.

'One of them had passed out and woken up on a mattress, naked and covered in cigarette burns and bites. The other girl was raped in his car in the countryside before she was thrown out in the middle of nowhere and left to find her own way home.'

My heart was pounding. This all sounded horribly familiar.

'The girls were both told there were films of them being raped, and if they didn't do what this man said, he would post them online and show them to everyone they knew,' continued Emma. 'Eventually he gave them mobile phones and forced them into delivering drugs for him to other towns on the train. He said young girls like them were less likely to be stopped by police.

'They were only fourteen years old, Maggie,' she sighed. 'Two young, vulnerable girls in the care system who had no one looking out for them.

'And when the police interviewed them, guess who they said was responsible for grooming them, raping them, degrading them in the most unimaginable way and then forcing them to be his drugs mules?'

I felt sick to my stomach because I knew exactly what she was going to say next.

'Lenny West,' she sighed.

The man who had done the same thing to Hannah well over a year before. My worst fears had been confirmed.

What a monster.

'But there is some good news,' Emma told me. 'This time, because the girls were found straight afterwards, there is forensic evidence linking Lenny to the attack.

'They've charged him, Maggie.'

'That's brilliant news,' I gasped. 'He'll finally be brought to justice.'

'At the moment, DC Williams says it looks like he's going to plead not guilty so there's going to be a trial,' continued Emma. 'So that's why I've come to see you.'

She explained that the police wanted to re-interview Hannah and go through her statement with her. There was also the possibility that she might be called to give evidence.

'I know this will be a huge bombshell for her and I didn't just want to ring her and tell her over the phone,' sighed Emma. 'I feel it's something I need to do face to face. I know she has a good relationship with you, so I wanted to ask if you'd consider coming to Devon with me to talk to her. I think it would really help. We could go there and back in the same day.'

My head was spinning as I tried to take everything in. My main worry was the effect this news was going to have on Hannah. I had no idea how she was going to react, especially now that she was finally starting to rebuild her life. I knew, whatever she felt about it, it was going to be a huge shock.

'Of course I'll come with you,' I told Emma. 'If you think it would help.'

Emma explained that she'd already had a chat with my supervising social worker, Becky, who was happy for me to go to Devon with Emma if I wanted to.

'What I have to do now though is give Shelley a call and break the news to her,' Emma told me.

'Good luck,' I told her.

That poor family had been through so much and, as with Hannah, I didn't know how Shelley she was going to react to this new bombshell.

I spent the rest of the day lost in my own thoughts. My head was all over the place – a mixture of worry about Hannah, and anger that Lenny had been free to do these horrendous things to other vulnerable young girls.

Emma called me back the following morning.

'I spoke to Shelley,' she said. 'It was quite a shock for her and understandably, like you and me, she's worried about the effect this is going to have on Hannah.

'Apparently she's starting to make good progress with her counselling and is starting to open up a bit more, but Shelley's worried that this will make her go into herself again. Equally though, she thinks that knowing Lenny is being brought to justice might help her.'

'We won't know until we tell her, I suppose,' I sighed.

Emma and Shelley agreed that Shelley would let Hannah know that we were coming to visit but she was just going to say it was to see how she was getting on. We agreed that we'd drive to Devon in three days' time. Shelley could finish work early and we'd be there when Hannah got home from school.

Over the next couple of days, I walked around in a daze. On the one hand, I was looking forward to seeing Hannah again after so long, but I was also worried about what this news might do to her.

'I'm going to be out all day on Wednesday,' I told Shola. 'I've got to go and visit a girl I used to foster last year and I won't be back until later.'

'No problem, Maggie – Phoenix and I will be fine,' she smiled.

She was going to a mother and baby group in the morning and I arranged for Vicky to call round in the afternoon to keep her company.

On Wednesday morning, Emma came to pick me up. My stomach was churning with nerves as I saw her car pull up outside.

'How are you, Maggie?' she asked as I got into the passenger seat.

'If I'm being completely honest, I'm dreading this,' I said. 'Hannah's been through so much, I just hope this doesn't tip her over the edge.'

It was a long journey and Emma and I chatted and listened to the radio. I'd never spent that much time alone with her and it was nice to get to know her better. We talked about the house she'd just bought with her boyfriend and the cat they'd adopted, which helped take my mind off the task that lay ahead of us.

Hours later we finally arrived in the town – a pretty place with a harbour and a few shops in the centre. They had moved out of Shelley's brother's house by now, and were renting their own house.

'I think this is it,' said Emma, pulling up outside a row of townhouses on a new-build estate. As we walked up the front path, I felt the tingle of nerves. Shelley must have been looking out for us because before we could ring the bell, the door opened and she gave us both a hug.

'It's lovely to see you after all this time, Maggie,' she smiled.

'How's it going?' I asked her as she led us into the small but cosy kitchen and put the kettle on.

'It's been a big change but we love it here,' she said.

'And how's Hannah?' asked Emma.

Shelley sighed.

'I'm not going to lie, it's been hard for her,' she told us. 'Just because we've moved, it doesn't mean it all goes away.

'She finds it hard to trust people after what's happened, so she's struggled to make friends at school. She finds it difficult to concentrate and she's still way behind with her work.'

'It's understandable after everything she's been through, though,' I told her gently. 'It's going to take time.'

'She's started counselling, which seems to be helping. The panic attacks and the nightmares are getting less.'

Poor girl, I thought.

I was even more worried about what we were about to tell her. Would it bring all her trauma back?

Molly came in from school just after half past three.

'Do you mind giving us half an hour, love? Maggie and Emma need to talk to Hannah when she gets back.' Shelley told her, and Molly went upstairs to do her homework.

Hannah got home ten minutes later. She looked like a different girl. She was wearing hardly any make-up, she'd got a golden tan and she'd put on a bit of weight so she didn't look so painfully thin anymore.

'Hello lovey,' I smiled. 'It's so good to see you. How are you?'

'Alright,' she said shyly.

Shelley got her a drink of juice and encouraged her to sit with us at the table.

'How's school going?' Emma asked her.

'It's OK,' she said. 'It's been hard cos everybody knows each other and I'm really behind in my GCSEs, but I've made a couple of mates now.'

We chatted for a while and I looked at Emma, wondering when she was going to tell Hannah the real reason we were here. I could see Shelley was thinking the same thing.

'Hannah, Maggie and I wanted to come and see you today to talk about Lenny,' she told her at last.

Hannah flinched at the mention of his name.

'Why do you want to talk about him?' she snapped.

Emma explained how DC Williams had been in touch and then, very calmly, she told her what had happened to these two other girls.

Shelley had tears in her eyes as she listened to what they had been through.

Hannah looked stunned.

'What do you mean?' she asked. 'He did the same thing to them but he might actually go to prison this time?'

'Hopefully,' said Emma. 'The police believe they have enough evidence this time around to secure a conviction. So they want to talk to you again about what he did to you so they can use your evidence to strengthen the case against him.'

Hannah buried her head in her hands and I could see that she was struggling to take it all in.

'I can't do it,' she mumbled. 'I don't want to talk about it anymore.'

With that, she pushed her chair back from the table and ran out of the room.

We all looked at each other, none of us sure what to do next.

'I'll go and talk to her if you'd like?' I suggested.

Emma nodded and Shelley just looked shell-shocked.

Hannah was in the front room curled up in a ball on the sofa.

I sat down next to her.

'I know this must be a big shock for you, lovey,' I told her. 'It was a big shock for all of us. But this is good news, Hannah. They might be able to get him this time, and then he won't be able to hurt anyone ever again.'

Hannah sat up, her blue eyes filled with tears.

'Why do the police believe those girls and they didn't believe me, Maggie?' she asked.

'They did believe you, Hannah,' I replied. 'We all did. There just wasn't enough evidence to be able to take Lenny to court.

'But now there is, and hopefully that will mean that he'll get locked up for a very long time.'

'Will I have to go to court?'

'You might do,' I nodded. 'No one can say for certain just yet. All we know is that the police want to go through your statement with you again and then they'll take it from there.'

There was also one other thing that we hadn't had a chance to mention yet.

'The offences that Lenny has been charged with are so serious that the judge refused to give him bail,' I told her.

'What does that mean?' she asked.

'It means that he's currently in prison and he'll have to stay there until the court case.'

'So he's locked up?' she asked, sounding shocked.

I nodded.

That news seemed to help calm Hannah down and I managed to persuade her to come back into the kitchen.

'How are you feeling, darling?' asked Shelley.

She shrugged.

'Scared,' she sighed. 'And worried.'

'Well you don't have to do this on your own,' Shelley told her. 'I'll drive us up there and I'll come to the police station and sit with you when they're doing the interview.'

Hannah scowled.

'But I don't think I can say all those things in front of you,' she sighed. 'I don't want you to hear what he did to me. Please can Maggie come with me instead? She was with me the last time.'

'I'm afraid I'm not your foster carer anymore, flower, so it's not really the done thing,' I told her.

'Please, Maggie,' she begged, her eyes filling with tears again.

I looked at Emma for guidance.

'If Maggie is happy to, then I'm sure we can sort something out,' she replied.

Hannah looked relieved.

'When do the police want to see her?' asked Shelley.

'As soon as possible,' replied Emma. 'The next few days would be ideal.'

'That soon?' asked Hannah, her eyes wide with fear.

I could see she was scared out of her wits but somehow we had to get her through this and then finally perhaps she could get some justice.

SEVENTEEN

Facing Fear

Sunlight glinted off the glass and dazzled me as I stood on the pavement. This police station couldn't have been more different from the last one. Whereas the last one was an old, rundown Victorian brick building, this one was newly built and gleaming with bright blue panels and huge glass windows. The bright surroundings still didn't make what we were about to do any easier, though.

As I waited outside for Shelley and Hannah to arrive, I felt a sinking feeling in the pit of my stomach. I was nervous about how today was going to go. It had been nearly fourteen months since Hannah had last been interviewed about the ordeal she had been through with Lenny. Throughout those months she'd endured nightmares, panic attacks and days when she didn't want to leave the house. But as time had gone on, things had slowly got a little easier. I knew that we were all worried that being interviewed by the police, having to go over every little thing in minute detail again, was going to bring it all back and leave her feeling more traumatised than ever.

I looked at my watch – we were ten minutes late for our appointment. I knew they'd had an early start as Shelley had texted me when they'd set off from Devon. She'd borrowed her brother's car so they could travel there and back the same day so Hannah didn't miss too much school.

At last, I saw them crossing the road by the car park. As they walked towards me, Hannah looked very sullen and serious, but Shelley gave me a little wave and a weak smile.

'How are you doing?' I asked.

'A little bit tired,' replied Shelley. 'It was a long journey but we're here now.'

'And what about you, Hannah?' I asked.

She shrugged her shoulders.

'How long is this going to take?' she sighed.

'I don't honestly know, sweetie,' I told her. 'Let's go in and talk to DC Williams.'

I could see she was nervous, but that was understandable.

Hannah and Shelley sat in reception while I went to the front desk and explained we were there to see DC Williams.

A few minutes later she came out. She was wearing a smart black trouser suit as she was in CID now and didn't have to wear a uniform.

'Hello Maggie,' she smiled at me, shaking my hand. 'Thanks so much for coming. Where's Hannah?' she asked, clearly worried that she hadn't come.

'She's sitting with her mum over there,' I said. 'I think she's feeling very anxious about talking about all of this again.'

'I'll do my best to make this as comfortable as possible for her,' DC Williams told me. 'She's not accused of anything, it's purely to go through her statement and check all the details.

We just want to make sure everything is in order for the prosecutor before Lenny West's trial.' She paused and lowered her voice. 'In confidence, I also wanted to let you know that West is also facing several drugs charges,' she added.

She explained that when police had searched his flat, they had found large quantities of drugs, several mobile phones and a substantial amount of cash.

'He's going to face a separate court case for those offences as he's being charged with two other people in relation to the drugs so the CPS wanted to split the charges into separate court cases.'

It was a lot to take in.

DC Williams and I walked over to where Hannah and Shelley were sitting.

'Hi Hannah,' she said softly. 'It's nice to see you again.'

Hannah remained stony-faced. To be honest, I wasn't surprised. The last time she had seen this woman she'd been interrogating her, and I could see DC Williams was aware of that.

'Right, let's take you all through,' she told us.

'I want Maggie to come with me and not Mum,' Hannah said firmly, not looking at us.

I felt a bit awkward, but I could see Shelley was putting a brave face on things.

'If that's what you want, Han, then I'm happy to go along with it,' she told her. 'I'll be out here waiting for you.

'Thanks Maggie,' she said to me.

I could see Hannah was nervous as DC Williams led us down a warren of corridors.

'Here we are,' she said, opening the door to an interview room.

It was so much nicer than the room Hannah had been taken to before. There were big windows and it was light and airy. Instead of threadbare, hard blue office chairs there were four comfy armchairs and a table. The only thing that signified it was an interview room was the tape recorder on the side.

DC Williams took out a large file of papers and started to sort through them.

'Right, shall we make a start?' she asked.

'Why do you believe me now but you didn't believe me last time?' Hannah blurted out suddenly.

'Hannah, we've always believed you,' DC Williams told her earnestly. 'I've never forgotten about you and everything you went through.

'I was so frustrated that we couldn't take it further at the time, but we have to go on the CPS's recommendations. It wouldn't have been fair on you to pursue it only for Lenny to get let off. But now we've got two other girls who are telling us similar stories and this time we do have forensic evidence.

'I really need your help to try and make sure Lenny West goes to prison for a very long time for what he's done to you all. OK?'

Hannah nodded.

Slowly and methodically, DC Williams went through Hannah's statement line by line detailing all the horrendous things she went through. Hearing it again was just as horrific as the first time.

Her whole body was trembling as she recalled how Lenny had drugged and raped her multiple times.

'Do you want to take a break or have a drink?' DC Williams asked her.

Hannah shook her head.

'No, I want to carry on,' she said bravely, tears streaming down her face.

It was horrible to see her so visibly distressed and I reached across the table for her hand to try and comfort her. She grabbed it in a vice-like grip and squeezed it as DC Williams asked her about the night that she was dumped in the countryside.

'He burnt me with cigarettes and said I had to do as he said, otherwise he'd rape Molly,' she wept.

At the mention of her sister, she dissolved into big gulping sobs.

'I'm going to pause there for a minute,' said DC Williams gently, handing her a box of tissues.

Hannah pulled one out with a trembling hand.

'You're doing so well,' I told her. 'It will all be over soon.'

Just over an hour after we'd arrived at the police station, it finally was.

'Hannah, you've been incredibly brave going through all that again with me,' DC Williams told her.

Hannah's eyes were swollen and red and her face was drained of colour.

'What happens now?' I asked.

DC Williams explained that the files were being prepared for the CPS and they would be in touch with a court date.

'We'll keep your social worker updated,' she told Hannah gently.

'Will Hannah have to give evidence at court?' I asked.

'At this stage I very much doubt it but again I'll let you know if that changes.'

DC Williams walked us out to reception. Shelley was sitting waiting for us, and as soon as she saw Hannah and the state she was in, she rushed over to her.

'Oh love,' she sighed, and Hannah collapsed into her arms, sobbing.

'It was horrible, Mum,' she sobbed.

'It's all over now,' Shelley soothed, stroking her long hair.

Before they drove back, we'd arranged to meet Emma at Social Services.

'Are you sure you feel up to it?' Shelley asked, her brow furrowed in concern as we left the police station.

'I'm OK,' nodded Hannah. 'It's over now, so I feel better.'

At Social Services, we went into a spare meeting room and Emma brought us all a cup of tea.

'How did it go?' she asked.

'Hannah did brilliantly and was very brave,' I told her.

Emma gave her a sympathetic smile.

'DC Williams is going to keep in touch with us and let us know when the trial is,' I went on.

'Maggie and I will keep in touch with you both and let you know what the outcome is,' Emma told them, but Hannah shook her head.

'No way. I want to be there,' she said firmly. 'I want to be there at the court to see him get punished.'

I looked at Emma.

'Hannah, I really don't think that's a good idea,' she told her. 'Hopefully that's what will happen but there's always a risk that Lenny could be found not guilty too.'

'I don't care,' she replied. 'I want to go. I want to see him.'

'Let's see how you feel nearer the time,' Shelley told her, clearly hoping that she would change her mind. Hannah nodded, but her face was set. She suddenly looked much older than her fifteen years.

Before long, it was time for Shelley and Hannah to set off back to Devon. I gave them both a goodbye hug.

'You look after yourself,' I told Hannah. 'And keep in touch.'

She nodded.

Once they'd gone, I stayed behind for a quick chat with Emma.

'Hopefully she'll change her mind about going to court,' I told her. 'It will set her right back again and she'll feel that she's not been believed all over again.'

'Hopefully that outcome is unlikely but we both know that nothing is guaranteed, even with forensics,' nodded Emma. 'Things happen in court cases and juries make decisions that you don't expect or understand.'

'It is a risk, but as long as we've explained that risk to Hannah, there's not much else that we can do,' I sighed. 'We have to respect her decision.'

Maybe she was facing her fears. And her fear was Lenny West.

EIGHTEEN

Justice

Over the next few weeks, the court case loomed large over all of us. Hannah texted regularly, mainly to ask if there had been any update from the court.

Then finally one day DC Williams contacted me.

We have a date for the trial, I texted Shelley. *Emma will call and give you all the details.*

It had been two months since Hannah had gone over her statement with the police and she hadn't changed her mind about being at the verdict. I'd talked to her and so had Emma and Shelley, but she'd resolutely stuck to her guns.

'I spoke to her counsellor about it and she said if that's what Hannah wants to do then we should support her,' Shelley had told me. 'It's all part of her recovery process and I think she needs to face him.'

I still felt worried about what impact seeing Lenny again might have on Hannah.

I didn't sleep much in the days leading up to the court case.

'What are you doing up, Maggie? Is everything OK?' Shola asked when she bumped into me on the landing one night at 2 a.m. She was up with Phoenix, who was teething, and she'd heard me padding about. As expected, Shola had passed her parenting assessment with flying colours, and she and Phoenix were now just waiting for the local authority to house them.

'I'm OK, lovey,' I told her. 'I've just got a lot on my mind.'

I hadn't told her about Hannah and the court case as I always tried to keep information about other children confidential.

The trial was expected to last a week and every day, DC Williams texted Emma and I with updates from court.

Girls have given evidence by video link. Went well. Handled cross-examination brilliantly.

Lenny's not taking the stand.

Closing statements from defence and prosecution.

Judge giving her summing up.

And then finally after eleven days: *Jury has gone out to consider their verdict.*

As soon as I got the text, I rang Shelley.

'It's happening,' I told her. 'The jury has gone out.'

'I know, I just got a message from Emma,' she said. 'I feel sick, Maggie.

'Are we doing the right thing coming to court?'

'It's what Hannah wants, and I think we have to respect that,' I told her.

The jury had only gone out late that afternoon and they were unlikely to come back the same day, so Shelley and Hannah were going to drive up that evening.

Hannah had already asked if she could stay at my house, which was fine, but Shelley wasn't able to because I had Shola and Phoenix living with me and she wasn't police checked.

'I honestly don't mind, I'll stay with a friend,' she'd told me on the phone. 'It might be for the best. I know Hannah always listens to you and you're good at keeping her calm.'

It was late by the time they arrived that night.

'Come on in,' I whispered to them both, so as not to wake Phoenix and Shola, who were asleep upstairs.

We arranged to meet Shelley at court in the morning.

'Bye darling, I love you,' she said to Hannah, giving her a kiss. 'Try and get some sleep.'

I made Hannah a cup of tea before she went to bed.

'How are you feeling about tomorrow?' I asked her.

She shrugged her shoulders.

'One minute I'm OK and the next I'm really scared,' she told me. 'I just want it to be over and Lenny to be locked up in prison.'

'Well hopefully the jury will agree with you,' I told her, giving her a sympathetic smile.

I took her upstairs with her overnight bag.

'You're in your old bedroom,' I smiled. 'I've got it all ready for you.'

I'd already explained about Shola and Phoenix being in the other bedroom.

When she'd got ready for bed, I went in to say goodnight.

She lay there looking terrified. It's often at bedtime when children's worries and anxieties come out and I could see reality had hit Hannah.

She was going to court tomorrow to face the man who had groomed her, split her from her family, raped and hurt her.

I sat down on the bed and put my hand on her arm.

'Hannah, there's one thing I need you to know,' I told her. 'If you wake up tomorrow morning and you don't want to go to court, you don't have to. You can change your mind at any point and it will be absolutely fine,' I added. 'No one's going to think any less of you. I'm willing to go to court for you if you don't want to.'

'I know,' she sighed. 'Everyone keeps telling me that but honestly I'm not going to change my mind. I can do it, Maggie. I want to do it.'

She was a very strong, determined young woman but that still didn't stop me from worrying about her.

I knew I wouldn't be able to sleep if I went to bed, so to take my mind off things, I stayed up to watch a film. My plan worked. I was so exhausted by the time I went to bed, I must have nodded straight off. The next thing I knew, my alarm was going off and it was 6.30 a.m. I was surprised when I went downstairs to find Hannah in the kitchen. She was already dressed and making toast.

'Would you like a slice, Maggie?' she asked.

'Well, this is very nice, getting breakfast made for me,' I smiled. 'You'll have to come and stay more often.'

I could see that she was using the same coping mechanism I relied on, of keeping busy and finding things to do so she didn't have time to dwell on what was going to happen today. When Shola came down with Phoenix, I introduced them. The baby was a welcome distraction and Hannah cooed over her.

An hour later, it was time to leave. The court was over an hour's drive from my house and I'd never been there before. The crown courts I'd been to in the past tended to be ornate Victorian buildings with pillars outside and wood-panelled court rooms, but this one was an ugly, sprawling 1980s brick building. Emma and Shelley were already standing outside waiting for us when we arrived.

'How are you holding up?' Shelley asked Hannah, going over and putting her arm around her.

'I'm OK, Mum,' Hannah replied, giving her a brave smile. 'I was in my old bedroom at Maggie's and I managed to get some sleep.'

As we walked into the atrium and waited to go through the security scanners, I felt a knot of anxiety in my stomach. Courts were such serious, formal places they always made me nervous. I was also worried at how Hannah was going to cope with seeing Lenny again.

'So, now we wait,' smiled Emma once we'd all got through. 'Let's find somewhere to sit and I'll get us all a drink. DC Williams said she'll be along later.'

That was the other issue. Even though the jury had gone out, we didn't know how long their deliberations were going to take. They could be out for days. We had to prepare ourselves for a lot of waiting around. We found a spare place to sit on some uncomfortable plastic seats and Emma went and got us all a coffee from a vending machine.

'How are you doing?' I asked Hannah.

'Will everyone stop asking if I'm alright?' she snapped.

'Maggie just wants to make sure you're OK, darling,' Shelley told her gently. 'We all do. We're all worried about you.'

'Well, I'm fine,' she sighed.

A couple of hours passed. Hannah flicked through her phone, Emma did some work and Shelley and I chatted for a bit. The waiting was torture. I found myself tearing my polystyrene coffee cup into small pieces to pass the time.

Shelley wanted to nip outside for a cigarette so we left Emma with Hannah and I went with her for some fresh air.

'How are you coping with all of this?' I asked her.

She shrugged and took a drag on her cigarette.

'I don't know how I'm going to feel when I see him,' she sighed. 'I'm worried I'll want to leap over the dock and kill him for what he did to my little girl.'

I knew all of this was hard for her too and she still blamed herself for what had happened to Hannah.

Three hours of waiting later and it was lunchtime. All of the courts adjourned for an hour and we knew the jury wouldn't come back in that time, so we walked into the town centre to get a sandwich. When we arrived back at court, DC Williams was there.

'What's happened?' gasped Hannah. 'Have they decided?'

'Not yet, I'm afraid,' she told her.

She sat with us so she could answer any questions that we might have.

'Will that man be able to see us when we're sitting in court?' asked Shelley nervously.

She couldn't even bring herself to use his name.

'We'll be sitting in the public gallery, which is on an upper level behind the dock where West will be stood,' explained DC Williams. 'He won't even know that you're there, but even if he wanted to see you, he'd have to turn right around in his seat and look up.'

'I don't mind,' said Hannah defiantly. 'I don't care if he sees me. I'm not scared of him anymore.'

DC Williams talked Hannah and Shelley through how the jury would come back and the judge would ask the spokesperson to read out their verdicts.

'Are the other girls here?' asked Hannah. 'The other ones he hurt?'

DC Williams shook her head.

'They gave their evidence earlier in the trial via video link so they wouldn't be able to see West. They did well but understandably, it was very traumatic for them and they didn't want to come back to court for the verdict.

'Everyone has their own way of handling things.'

Hannah looked disappointed.

Another two hours passed in a blur of shifting on uncomfortable seats and horrible vending machine drinks. I think we'd all resigned ourselves to the fact that nothing was going to happen today when suddenly an announcement came over the tannoy.

'Will all parties in the case of Lenny West please go to Court Two, where the court will resume in twenty minutes.'

Shelley jumped up out of her seat and Emma and I looked at each other in shock. DC Williams promptly headed off to the courtroom and we told her we would follow shortly.

'This is really happening, isn't it?' muttered Hannah.

She'd been so calm all day, but now that the moment had come, she looked ashen.

'Come on, lovey, it's time to go,' I told her gently.

She stood up, but as she did, her legs buckled and she grabbed hold of the plastic seat.

'I don't feel well,' she mumbled, sinking back down again. 'I'm all dizzy and I can't breathe.'

She was gasping for breath and I knew the signs. She was having a panic attack.

'Keep breathing in and out,' I told her gently, rubbing her back.

Shelley and Emma looked on, their faces crumpled with worry.

'You can do it,' I told Hannah calmly. 'That's it. Nice deep breaths in and out.'

'I'm scared,' she croaked. 'What if he gets off?'

'Try not to talk,' I told her. 'Just stay calm and keep breathing.'

'I know he was the one who broke Molly's arm, put the brick through my mum's window and tried to break in,' she panted. 'He always said he'd rape Molly if I told anyone what he'd done. What if he gets off?'

'There are no guarantees, but the police believe there's enough evidence to convict him so hopefully that's what's going to happen,' I told her. 'And whatever happens, you live hundreds of miles away now and there's no way Lenny knows where you are. We will all make sure of that.'

Hannah nodded but I wasn't sure if she truly believed it. Thankfully she stopped talking and gradually she seemed to calm down. Slowly, her breathing went back to normal and the colour came back into her cheeks.

'I don't want to rush you, Hannah, but if you want to be there for the verdict then we need to head into the court now,' said Emma gently, looking at her watch.

'This is the very last time I'm going to ask you this,' I said to Hannah. 'But are you sure that you want to do this?'

Hannah nodded.

'I'll be fine,' she said firmly. 'Let's go.'

We walked up the stairs to the entrance to the public gallery in Court Two where DC Williams was waiting for us.

'All OK?' she asked, and we nodded.

'They're just about to start,' she whispered.

There were only a couple of people in the gallery and I looked to Hannah for guidance over where she wanted to sit.

She walked straight to the front row. Emma went in first and Shelley and I sat either side of her.

It was a modern, brightly lit courtroom and I'd hardly had any time to take it all in when suddenly there was movement in the dock. A security guard appeared and I could see that they were bringing Lenny up from the holding cells. I felt Hannah stiffen beside me.

'Just keep breathing in and out,' I whispered to her. 'Remember he can't hurt you now.'

A figure was led into the dock flanked by two guards.

I couldn't see him properly because we were sitting behind him, as DC Williams had promised, but he was tall and broad-shouldered with sallow skin and greasy shoulder-length hair.

I hated this man for everything that he had done to Hannah. But when I saw him stood there in his baggy, grey prison-issue tracksuit, he just looked pathetic.

I gave Hannah a quick glance next to me, but her face was blank and emotionless.

All the barristers at the front stood up as the judge, a woman in her fifties, walked into court. Then she asked the spokesperson of the jury to stand up. He was a sensible-looking man with glasses in his thirties.

'Have you reached a decision?' she asked him.

Suddenly I could feel Hannah trembling next to me and I reached for her hand. I could see that Shelley had taken hold of her other hand.

'We have,' he nodded.

I shut my eyes and squeezed Hannah's hand tightly. My heart was pumping so much it felt like it was going to burst out of my chest.

Please let them make the right decision, I willed.

If they didn't, I had no idea how Hannah was going to cope.

'In the count of rape, how do you find the defendant?' asked the judge.

There was a pause.

I held my breath.

'Guilty.'

I let out a huge sigh of relief. Hannah was still staring straight ahead but I noticed a single tear roll down her cheek.

It was the same decision for the five rape charges that he had faced.

'Guilty.'

Everything seemed to happen quickly after that. Lenny slumped down in the dock and put his head in his hands. The judge retired and he was led back down to the cells. The barristers started packing their files away and the court ushers left.

'He got what he deserved,' hissed Shelley.

Hannah just sat there, looking stunned.

'Does that mean he's going to prison?' she asked.

'Yes,' I nodded. 'Hopefully for a very long time.'

DC Williams explained it would be a few weeks until Lenny was sentenced but she would come to court and let us know how long he got.

'Thank you for being so brave,' she told Hannah. 'Your statement helped strengthen our case and make sure he got put away for what he did to you and those other girls.'

Hannah didn't say anything and I could tell that she was in shock. I was just utterly relieved that the jury had found him guilty. The alternative was unthinkable.

It was a different, lighter mood as we came out of court. We chatted and laughed as we walked down the corridor. I suddenly noticed Hannah wasn't with us, so I turned around to see she was lagging behind.

'Are you OK, flower?' I asked her.

Her face told me that she wasn't. I walked towards her and she collapsed into my arms, sobbing her heart out. As I held her, her body shook with hot, gulping sobs. I think the trauma of the past eighteen months, every horrific thing she had been through, had suddenly hit her.

'They believed me,' she cried. 'Now everyone knows he's a bad man.'

'Of course they believed you, sweetie,' I soothed. 'We all do. He's going to be locked up for a long, long time and he can't hurt you or anyone else ever again.'

'I know,' she sniffed, wiping away her tears. 'It doesn't seem real.'

I knew the reality would take a long time to sink in.

'Oh Han,' sighed Shelley, giving her a hug. 'Come on, let's get you out of here.'

I had such a feeling of relief as we walked out of court into the crisp winter afternoon sun.

'Well, I must get back to the office,' said Emma. 'But I'll be in touch.'

She gave Hannah and Shelley a hug before she went to her car.

'Would you like to come back to my house for a coffee, or go and get something to eat before you head off?' I asked Shelley and Hannah.

Shelley shook her head.

'We have to get back I'm afraid, Maggie. Molly's at a friend's house so we have to pick her up and both girls have got school tomorrow.'

I understood but it seemed like such an abrupt end to what had been a traumatic day.

'Well, I guess this is goodbye then,' I said.

I did my best to stay upbeat, but my words caught in my throat.

'You take care of yourself,' I whispered to Hannah as I gave her a hug. 'You've been so brave and so strong and I'm so, so proud of you.'

'Thank you for everything, Maggie,' she smiled.

I gave Shelley a hug too.

'There are no words to say how grateful I am for everything you've done for me and for Hannah, Maggie,' she told me. 'You've got us through what's been the worst time of our lives.'

'I'm glad that I could help in some little way,' I told her, meaning it.

I did my best 'bright and breezy' act as I walked them to their car and cheerfully waved them off. It was only when I got into my own car that my mask crumbled and the tears flowed. I cried all the way home. My tears were for so many reasons – relief, tiredness, anger for what had been done to Hannah but most of all, a genuine sense of loss and sadness. My instincts told me that I probably wasn't going to see Hannah again.

Three weeks passed, and then one day, Emma rang me. DC Williams had contacted her to say Lenny West was going to be sentenced later that week.

'Do you mind if I go to the sentencing?' I asked her. 'I'd like to be in court for it so that I can tell Hannah what happened.'

'Not at all,' she told me.

I suppose it was the final piece of the puzzle. I wanted to see this man be punished for everything he had done to these girls, and I wanted to be able to tell Hannah all about it and answer her questions.

This time there was no waiting around. I sat in the public gallery and listened as the judge made her sentencing remarks. Lenny stood in the dock, his head slumped, as she addressed him.

'You took advantage of vulnerable young girls for your own sexual gratification and abused their trust in the most horrifying of ways,' she told him.

'You groomed them, gave them presents and showered them with compliments so they believed that they were in a genuine relationship with you.

'They loved and cared for you and believed that you were their boyfriend, then you plied them with drugs and alcohol before subjecting them to the most horrific abuse over a number of months.

'If they didn't comply then they were beaten up or threatened. I can't even begin to imagine the fear these children must have felt because of you.'

She sentenced Lenny West to twelve years in prison for five counts of rape. He shook his head as he was led down to the cells.

I walked out of court and sat on a bench outside and called Hannah to tell her.

'Good,' she said calmly. 'He got what he deserved.'

It was finally over, but I knew it would never be over for Hannah. What Lenny had done to her was going to affect her for the rest of her life. But hopefully this would be the start of her being able to move on.

Epilogue

I scanned the kitchen for anything that belonged to Shola.

'You've forgotten the steriliser,' I shouted upstairs. 'And your plastic plates and spoons.'

'Can you put them in the cardboard box please, Maggie?' Shola yelled down from upstairs.

Shola and Phoenix had finally been given their own place and were packing everything up, ready for their move to a two-bedroom flat half an hour away from me. I was going to be sad to see them go but I could see how excited Shola was to be starting a new life on her own with her daughter. She'd proved to us all she was a great mum and she certainly didn't need me looking over her shoulder. Social Services would still be keeping in touch with her and would be there to offer her help and support if she ever needed it.

I was always heavy-hearted when children left my home. It didn't seem like more than two minutes since I'd said goodbye to Hannah. We still kept in touch, mainly by text. In the past two months, Lenny West had been back at the crown court to face the drugs charges. I hadn't gone this time, but DC Williams had kept us all updated. He and three associates had pleaded guilty to conspiracy to supply class A drugs and had been sentenced to seven years each. In West's case, the judge ruled that his sentence should be served consecutively with his sentence for rape – meaning the time he was given for the drugs charges would be added to the time he was serving for rape. It meant he was going to spend the next nineteen years behind bars.

Later that day, before I drove Shola and Phoenix to their new flat, I checked my emails to find a new message. It was from Hannah and when I clicked on it, I could see she had sent me a photograph.

It was a picture of Shelley, Molly and Hannah in front of a familiar harbour.

We went back to Spain again, she had written. *It was great.*

Hannah was standing in her shorts and T-shirt with a big smile on her face. She was tanned, her face had filled out a little bit and she looked happy.

She wasn't the same carefree, innocent girl that she had been in the photo taken in the same spot two years before. I knew she would never be that girl again. But she was a strong young woman, and I knew she was determined not to let Lenny win, not to be defined by what had happened to her. I was still in awe of her resilience and bravery. When she'd first come to me, none of us had had any idea that she was being groomed and abused in the most horrendous way. But she'd carried on fighting and, despite being unfairly punished herself, she'd finally seen Lenny brought to justice for what he'd done. My eyes filled with tears as I looked at the young girl in the photo. Hannah had her whole life ahead of her now. I knew it might take years, but in time, I hoped that the wounds caused by Lenny would finally start to heal, and she could begin building a new life for herself.

Afterword

Hannah's story happened several years ago, at a time when I knew very little about grooming and exploitation. Now, because of scandals in places like Rochdale and other cities in the Midlands and North where thousands of young girls were groomed, raped and sexually abused by gangs of older men over a number of years, Social Services, the police and schools are much more aware of it, as are us foster carers. As part of our mandatory training, we're taught to spot the signs of grooming and immediately report any concerns.

Looking back, I also realise that what happened to Hannah was one of the early cases of what is now known as 'county lines'. This is where gang members recruit vulnerable people, often children, to move or sell drugs from big cities to towns and more rural or coastal areas. They sell the drugs via mobile phones then use threats, violence and sexual abuse to force children into storing and delivering the drugs along with weapons and cash.

It's something I've become increasingly aware of in the past couple of years and sadly it seems to be a growing phenomenon. The National Crime Agency (NCA) estimates profits from the trade nationwide are around £500 million a year and a recent report by the Children's Society found the main age bracket for children being exploited is fourteen to seventeen, but that children as young as seven are being targeted by county lines dealers.

It's absolutely horrifying, but what I do know is that if Hannah was in my care now and the same thing happened, she would be treated very differently by the police and the authorities. There are guidelines in place now so if children have been forced to sell drugs in county lines operations, the CPS are encouraged not to prosecute them. The Modern Slavery Act gives young people and vulnerable adults the right to raise a defence which states that they were trafficked and forced to commit the offences. Sadly it's too late for Hannah but I take comfort from the fact that another child shouldn't have to go through what she did and have the fear of being charged with a criminal offence and going to court hanging over their heads when they've already been through so much. It breaks my heart when I read about similar stories in the newspaper or hear them from fellow foster carers and I often think of Hannah and wonder how she's doing. I wanted to tell her story in the hope that the more people are aware that this is going on, the more likely we are to stop this happening to another child.

Acknowledgements

Thank you to my children, Tess, Pete and Sam, who are such a big part of my fostering today; however, I had not met you when Hannah came into my home. To my wide circle of fostering friends – you know who you are! Your support and your laughter are valued. To my friend Andrew B for your continued encouragement and care. Thanks also to Heather Bishop, who spent many hours listening and enabled this story to be told, my literary agent Rowan Lawton and to Anna Valentine and Marleigh Price at Trapeze for giving me the opportunity to share these stories.

DADDY'S LITTLE SOLDIER

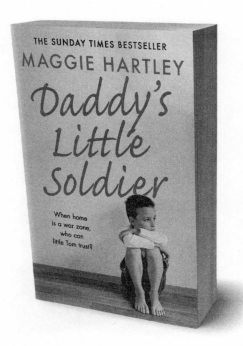

Tom has been taken into care following concerns that his dad is struggling to cope after the death of Tom's mum. When Maggie meets Tom's dad Mark, a stern ex-soldier and strict disciplinarian, it's clear that Tom's life at home without his mummy has been a constant battlefield. Can Maggie help Mark to raise a son and not a soldier? Or is little Tom going to lose his daddy too?

PLEASE, DON'T TAKE MY SISTERS

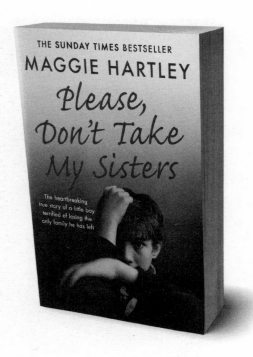

Leo's little sisters are the only family he has left in the world. But when Social Services begin to look at rehoming the little girls without their troubled older brother, the siblings' whole world comes crashing down. Can Maggie fight to keep the children together? Or will Leo lose the only love he's ever known?

A DESPERATE CRY FOR HELP

Meg arrives at Maggie's after a fire destroys the children's home she's been living in. But traumatised by the fire, and angry and vulnerable, having been put into care by her mother, Meg is lashing out at everyone around her. Can Maggie reach this damaged little girl before it's too late? And before Meg's destructive behaviour puts Maggie's life – and the lives of the other children in her care – at risk?

TINY PRISONERS

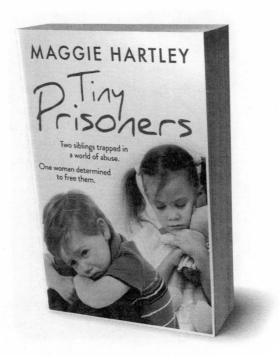

Evie and Elliot are scrawny, filthy and wide-eyed with fear when they turn up on foster carer Maggie Hartley's doorstep. They're too afraid to leave the house and any intrusion of the outside world sends them into a panic. It's up to Maggie to unlock the truth of their heart-breaking upbringing, and to help them learn to smile again.

THE LITTLE GHOST GIRL

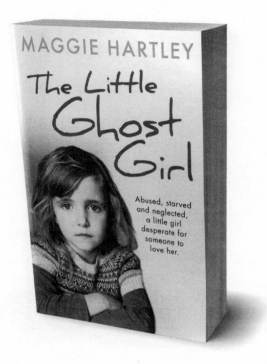

Ruth is a ghost of a girl when she arrives into foster mother Maggie Hartley's care. Pale, frail and withdrawn, it's clear to Maggie that Ruth had seen and experienced things that no 11-year-old should have to. Ruth is in desperate need of help, but can Maggie get through to her and unearth the harrowing secret she carries?

TOO YOUNG TO BE A MUM

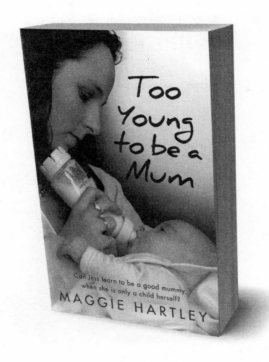

When sixteen-year-old Jess arrives on foster carer Maggie Hartley's doorstep with her newborn son Jimmy, she has nowhere else to go. With social services threatening to take baby Jimmy into care, Jess knows that Maggie is her only chance of keeping her son. Can Maggie help Jess learn to become a mum?

WHO WILL LOVE ME NOW?

At just ten years old, Kirsty has already suffered a lifetime of heartache and suffering. When her latest foster carers decide they can no longer cope, Kirsty comes to live with Maggie. Reeling from this latest rejection, the young girl is violent and hostile, and Social Services fear that she may be a danger to those around her. Maggie finds herself in an impossible position, one that calls into question her decision to become a foster carer in the first place...

BATTERED, BROKEN, HEALED

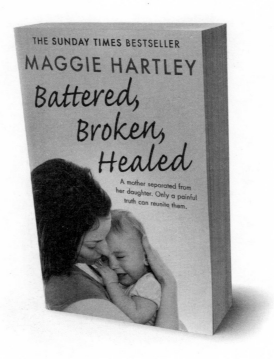

THE SUNDAY TIMES BESTSELLER

MAGGIE HARTLEY

Battered, Broken, Healed

A mother separated from her daughter. Only a painful truth can reunite them.

Six-week-old baby Jasmine comes to stay with Maggie after she is removed from her home. Neighbours have repeatedly called the police on suspicion of domestic violence, but her timid mother Hailey vehemently denies that anything is wrong. Can Maggie persuade Hailey to admit what's going on behind closed doors so that mother and baby can be reunited?

SOLD TO BE A WIFE

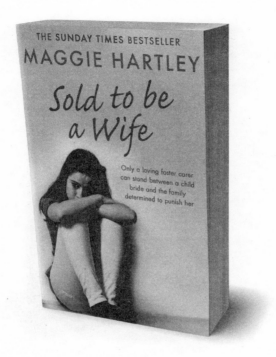

Fourteen-year-old Shazia has been taken into care over a fears that her family are planning to send her to Pakistan for an arranged marriage. But with Shazia denying everything and with social services unable to find any evidence, Shazia is eventually allowed to return home. But when Maggie wakes up a few weeks later in the middle of the night to a call from the terrified Shazia, it looks like her worst fears have been confirmed...

DENIED A MUMMY

THE SUNDAY TIMES BESTSELLER

MAGGIE HARTLEY

Denied a Mummy

The heartbreaking story of three little children searching for someone to love them

Maggie has her work cut out for her when her latest placement arrives on her doorstep; two little boys, aged five and seven and their eight- year-old sister. Having suffered extensive abuse and neglect, Maggie must slowly work through their trauma with love and care. But when a couple is approved to adopt the siblings, alarm bells start to ring. Maggie tries to put her own fears to one side but she can't shake the feeling of dread as she waves goodbye to them. Will these vulnerable children ever find a forever family?

TOO SCARED TO CRY

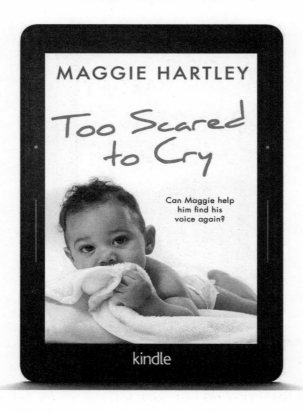

A baby too scared to cry. Two toddlers too scared to speak. This is the dramatic short story of three traumatised siblings, whose lives are transformed by the love of foster carer Maggie Hartley.

A FAMILY FOR CHRISTMAS

A tragic accident leaves the life of toddler Edward changed forever and his family wracked with guilt. Will Maggie be able to help this family grieve for the son they've lost and learn to love the little boy he is now? And will Edward have a family to go home to at Christmas?

THE GIRL NO ONE WANTED

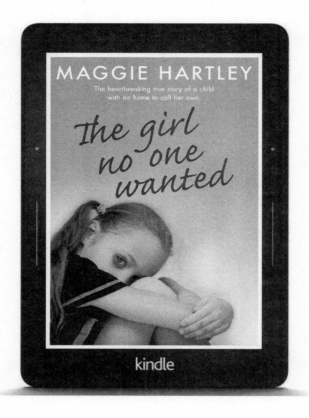

Eleven-year-old Leanne is out of control. With over forty placements in her short life, no local foster carers are willing to take in this angry and damaged little girl. Maggie is Leanne's only hope, and her last chance. If this placement fails, Leanne will have to be put in a secure unit. Where most others would simply walk away, Maggie refuses to give up on the little girl who's never known love.

IS IT MY FAULT MUMMY?

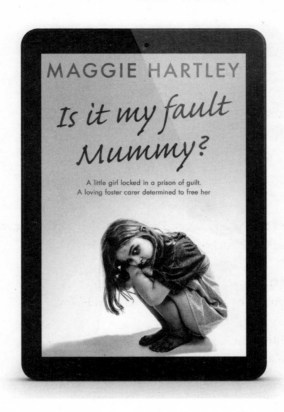

Seven-year-old Paris is trapped in a prison of guilt. Devastated after the death of her baby brother, Joel, Maggie faces one of the most heartbreaking cases yet as she tries to break down the wall of guilt surrounding this damaged little girl.

Credits

Maggie Hartley and Seven Dials would like to thank everyone at Orion who worked on the publication of *Exploited*.

Editorial
Marleigh Price

Copy editor
Clare Wallis

Proofreader
Helena Caldon

Audio
Paul Stark
Amber Bates

Contracts
Anne Goddard

Paul Bulos
Jake Alderson

Design
Rachael Lancaster
Joanna Ridley
Nick May

Editorial management
Jane Hughes
Alice Davis

Finance
Jasdip Nandra
Afeera Ahmed

Elizabeth Beaumont
Sue Baker

Marketing
Brittany Sankey

Production
Katie Horrocks

Publicity
Kate Moreton

Sales
Laura Fletcher
Esther Waters
Victoria Laws
Rachael Hum
Ellie Kyrke-Smith
Frances Doyle
Georgina Cutler

Operations
Jo Jacobs
Sharon Willis
Lisa Pryde
Lucy Brem